LOST ON HOPE ISLAND

The Amazing Tale
of the
Little Goat Midwives

Patricia Harman

Cover Art by Forest Harman
Illustrations by Trillium Stone

Flying Squirrel Press

ISBN # 978-0-9973941-0-8

Flying Squirrel Press
3011 Greystone Drive
Morgantown, West Virginia 26508

Layout and cover design: Liz Pavlovic
Cover art: Forest Harman
Editing: Dwight Pavlovic

DEDICATED TO THE CHILD IN ALL OF US
AND
INSPIRED BY MY GRANDCHILDREN
WHO, LIKE TRILLIUM AND JACOB,
ARE STRONG AND BRAVE AND KIND.

ACKNOWLEDGEMENTS

I would like to thank the many readers who got a first look at *Lost on Hope Island*. Some were midwives, some were parents, some were kids, some were goat people, some were friends, some were family. You know who you are. I am also grateful to Liz Pavlovic, who designed the book, Dwight Pavlovic who edited the book, and Forest Harman who did the cover art.

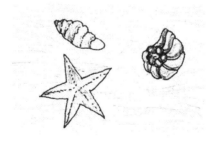

CHAPTER 1

ALONE

IN THE DREAM IT IS DARK. I hear screaming, then the roar of the wind and cold waves crashing over me. I'm in a sailboat and someone is holding me tight, someone familiar, maybe my mom, maybe my dad. No, it must be my mom, because in the dream I can see my father desperately dumping water over the boat's side. The boom almost hits him, but he ducks down. There's another smaller person in my mother's arms, but I can't see who it is because the spray is so heavy.

Then there's a jolt so hard it makes my teeth smash and the boat begins to fall apart. In the dream, which feels like the worst kind of nightmare, I hear myself scream then the water, dark, dark, and cold, sucks me down.

"Mom! Dad!" Salty liquid fills my mouth. I bob up again and see something floating in the moonlight. It's my brother. We grab each other and hold on, but the waves pull us down again.

When my head is out, I call for help. In the dream the dark water pulls my parents away from me, my parents who have always cared for me and made me feel safe.

When I wake, I can tell it's morning. I'm lying in the sand. Seagulls cry and a shadow moves across my face.

GRAY AND FORBIDDING

"Trillium?" a voice says. "Trillium, are you dead?" With great effort, I open my eyes and see a small boy on the beach. He's looking down, touching my arm with one running shoe.

"Noooo!" It irritates me to be touched like that and I inch away. "No, I'm not dead!" The boy, with brown skin and a dimple in his chin, very short dark curly hair and a dirty tear-streaked face, is my brother. He's only eight and sometimes, like now, he gets on my nerves.

Then I feel bad about it, because the little kid's scared. I'm scared too, but I'm older and should be kind. What bothers me most is my head feels so fuzzy and I still can't remember what actually happened.

"Here sit down next to me in the sand, Jacob. I'm sorry. Do you know where mom and dad are?"

"I can't find them," he sniffles. "I've been walking up and down the beach, but I don't know where they are. I can't find the boat either and I'm hungry. Our life jackets are over there."

I turn and see two puffy orange vests lying in the sand, but have no memory of taking mine off. "I want to go home," Jacob whimpers rubbing his eyes. "I'm hungry."

"I want to go home too," I tell him... but the truth is, I have no idea where home is. (I've heard that can happen, where after a blow to the head a person forgets everything.)

"Jacob? I know this sounds weird, but do you remember where we used to live?"

"America."

"But where in America?"

"Liberty, West Virginia, but dad took us camping on the beach."

"Where?"

"On the beach in Mexico. Don't you remember?"

Mexico? Why Mexico? But I give up trying to figure it out. My forehead hurts terribly and I have better things to do.

To stand, I lean on Jacob. He's little, but seems not to mind. Then we struggle up the steep gray cliff that shelters the beach. We have to find help.

All over the strange rocky land we hike, but we find no roads or stores, or houses anywhere. There are no sounds of machinery, radios, or human voices either. Black vultures with wings as wide as my arms circle above.

"Hello! Help!" We call until our throats hurt and our voices crack, but there's no answer and a queer emptiness overcomes me.

All we can see are mountains of gray and black rock, pitted with holes... small pointed cactus, short twisted pine trees and bushes with thorns. There are cracks in the rocks so wide and deep a person could fall into them and all around, in every direction, is water, gray and forbidding.

"I'm tired," whines Jacob "I don't want to explore anymore."

"We aren't exploring. We're looking for help. Do you see that...?" On the horizon, a blue-gray cloudbank is forming and lightning slashes the sky like a spear. "Another storm's coming." I pull him along, squeezing his little hand too tight. Jacob is small for his age and has skinny little legs and I know he's exhausted, but we have to find shelter before the rains come.

The kid plunks down on a rock and starts crying.

"I'm starving," he sobs. "I want Mama."

I care about my little brother, I do, but my head is pounding and I feel really mean. I jerk him up. He could at least try to act brave. I have to.

CHAPTER 2

by Trillium Stone

VOICES

"WHAT WAS THAT?" I whip my head around. Even sad little Jacob stands listening.

"It sounds like people," he says and we hurry in that direction.

"Beyaaaaa." The sounds get louder. "Beyaaaaa." If these are humans, they speak a different language. We look at each other, eyes wide, excited. Maybe there are adults who can give us food and maybe someone will have a cell phone. If they do, we can call our grandparents. I notice that I'm remembering more now and I can picture Grandma Jean and Grandpa Pete.

Grandma has curly red hair, like mine, only short and it bounces when she walks. She's a midwife who delivers babies in people's homes in West Virginia and lives on a farm on top of a mountain. Grandpa's hair is almost white. Even though he and my brother aren't related by birth, he has a dimple in his chin like Jacob and that makes them both happy.

Grandpa Pete is retired, but on his farm he has a cow, lots of chickens and a garden. Before he retired he taught science at the high school, so he knows all about plants and animals. He's also a musician and plays the guitar.

"Beyaaaaa, beyaaaaaaaa."

Jacob and I squeeze through another narrow opening between the big boulders and there on a ledge sits a massive billy goat. His long white beard hangs in strands down his chest and out of his head grow two enormous curved horns.

"Beeeyaaa!" he says looking down at us with flaming yellow eyes. "Beeeyaaa!" It's a nasal sound, like a sheep would make if it had a bad cold.

Below the billy, in a small clearing, are a herd of other goats, maybe thirty, maybe more. Some are big and some are little. Some have curved horns and some have only buds, but the billy goat is the biggest and smells the strongest too, like a wet dog, only worse. He stands, bleats another low warning out of his chest and Jacob hides behind me. "BEEYAAA!".

I don't know if we should run or act friendly, but I don't think we can get away fast enough, so I try talking softly like I would to a vicious dog.

"Niiice goat. Niiice Billy. Sorry to come into your home uninvited, but we're lost and need help. Are there any people around here?"

The billy goat makes a low sound again, lowers his head and shakes it. His eyes bore into mine and the other goats echo him in their higher voices.

Trying a different approach, I push Jacob in front of me. "Is there anything to eat? My poor little brother is hungry." How could the animal resist the little guy's tear streaked sad face?

One of the small goats prances up and butts Jacob in the chest. Then he jumps up on him with his front hooves, like a puppy. "Beyaaa!" he says. It's hard to tell if he's curious or trying to act friendly.

"Beyaaaaa," Jacob says, laughing, and all the goat's yellow eyes widen.

"Beyaaaaa?" they answer, because it sounds like Jacob's speaking their language.

King Billy (for in my mind that's what I now call the big fierce white goat with the long white beard) raises his enormous head with the curved horns and glares at his herd.

"Beyaaaa, beyaaaaaa, beyaaa," the little goats continue, moving forward and bumping Jacob with their noses. They're pushing him toward the edge of the clearing, but they stop under a grove of short twisty trees and start eating something.

For the first time, since we landed on the beach, we see food. There are strange, sweet smelling, knobby yellow fruit all over the ground, with bees buzzing over them. Jacob reaches down, picks one up, and starts to put it in his mouth. He isn't afraid of bees like I am.

"Stop! Jacob!" I run over and grab the fruit. "It might be poison!" My little brother looks like he might cry again, but he surprises me by saying something sensible. "I'm hungry and if the goats eat these, I think they're not poison."

"Poison will make you *die!*"

"I know! But this isn't poison. See the goats are fine." Before I can stop him, Jacob grabs another lumpy fruit and stuffs it in his mouth.

"See, it's good," he reports, the juice spilling down the cleft in his chin. "Not poison at all. I think poison would make your mouth hurt. These fruits are ugly, but they taste like pears... They have lots of seeds though." He laughs and spits them out. "Beyaaaa!" all the goats cry as if that's really funny.

I'm still suspicious, but as I carefully pick a ripe one

from the tree and take a tiny bite and then another, I find the fruit is sweet. "They're like figs, or maybe a little like pears."

by T.S.

King Billy is no longer threatening and has gone back to the highest rock, his guard post. He turns away and the other goats go back to their grazing, but the little ones stand around staring as if we're the new kids on the block.

I know what it feels like to be a new kid. It's coming back to me now. We've only lived in Liberty, West Virginia one year. Before that we lived in Ashville, North Carolina, where I had lots of friends, but Mom and Dad wanted to live closer to Grandpa and Gram, so we left it all. It made me sad, but sometimes in life, you just have to cope. If you ever find yourself lost at sea, you'll know what I mean. You could lie down and cry your eyes out, but if you want to survive, you just have to cope.

I sit down and lean against the rock wall to think. We're in a bad situation. My little brother rests on his back watching the kids play. They chase each other over the boulders and rise up on their hind legs in mock battle. He smiles his wide smile and looks like we're on a picnic. He doesn't look scared, but he should be.

THE TRAIL

The storm that had threatened moves on and the sun streaks out between the gray blue clouds.

"What are we going to do, Trillium?" Jacob turns to me.

"Well, for the moment, we're safe. We just have to wait it out a few days and I'm sure we'll be rescued, but we need water and then we need somewhere safe to spend the night."

"I have an idea." Jacob thinks out loud. "If we follow the goats, they'll know where good drinking water is. Maybe they belong to a farmer and they'll lead us back to his barn."

I'm surprised to find my little brother so sensible.

He may think, because I'm older, that I know what I'm doing, but the fact is I'm just putting one foot in front of the other, trying to go on, trying to stay alive.

"I like these goats," Jacob says. "They're the nicest ones I've ever met." This makes me smile, because, as far as I know, these are the only goats he's ever met, unless his other parents had goats, his first parents, before he came to us.

Jacob wasn't always my brother. He was born in Haiti and his parents were killed in that terrible earthquake that happened a few years ago. My father stole him. That's what dad says, but he laughs when he says it and it's only partly true.

250,000 people died in the quake and afterward that left a million orphans. Can you imagine? A million little kids without anyone to take care of them? Dad, who was on a photo shoot after the disaster, found Jacob, a little brown boy about two, wandering around in the rubble, half naked, tears running down his face. What else could he do? Walk on by? No, dad, who loves all children, just scooped him up, wrapped him in a blanket and took him back to the helicopter. Before he left Haiti, he went to a priest who filled out some papers and then they flew home.

At first mom was mad. She had just started back to

college to be a nurse midwife, but like dad she couldn't resist the little kid. After things settled down in Haiti, she wrote to the priest to see if any of Jacob's family had survived and the priest said no. So after piles of paper work, we got to adopt him and now he's my brother.

All afternoon, the herd moves slowly around and over boulders as big as delivery trucks. Sometimes the trail is well worn, other times you can't even see it. Between the rocks, in the shade, there are pockets of grass and on top of the rocks there are short twisty evergreens and fruit trees with the strange golden fruit.

The goats seem to eat everything, leaves and grass and weeds. As we follow them, Jacob and I keep looking for signs of other human life. We watch the gray water for boats. We listen for helicopters or search planes, but all we can hear is the bleating of goats, seagulls crying and the surf in the distance.

As the sun passes from east to west, I begin to feel more and more alone. Where are our parents? I don't want to think the unthinkable. All my life I'd been near them. Now they're gone, maybe at the bottom of the ocean. That's the part I can't think of.

"I wish I had some of their milk." Jacob breaks into my thoughts watching a little goat nurse from his mother. "I'm so thirsty."

"Maybe someday we can make friends with the mothers and they'll let us milk them." I say, but I don't like the way that sounds... "someday." I hope we aren't lost for that long.

CHAPTER 3

WATER

As the afternoon passed, Jacob and I became more and more thirsty. I looked at my brother and saw that his lips were peeling and dry. I licked mine and knew they were too.

"Trillium, you're getting burned," Jacob warned me. He knew I have freckles and can't take the sun.

"Yeah, but what can I do? We don't have hats or any suntan lotion." I tried to flop my hair over my face.

"How long can a person go without water before they die?" Jacob asked.

"I don't know and I don't want to think about it."

At last, the goats ambled down a narrow path between two huge gray-pitted rocks, to a little clearing where a pool of fresh water flowed out of the ground. It was a sight that made my heart sing.

Exhausted and thirsty, we waited our turn and when every goat had a long drink, we crawled forward. I let Jacob go first and then I dropped on my stomach and sucked up the cool liquid. We lay side-by-side and slurped up the water. For a moment we stopped and smiled and then we slurped some more. The water tasted better than lemonade, better than soda, better than anything. Finally we were full. We had a little

food, though the fruit wasn't much. We had water. That was important. Now we needed to find somewhere to sleep.

The animals were used to us now. As King Billy guarded the herd, the goats bedded down in twos and threes in the soft grass around the spring, so I took Jacob's hand and led him over to an empty place and sat down. It was getting dark and we had nowhere else to go. Tears formed at the corners of my eyes, but I wiped them away. If I started to cry, my little brother would too. In the distance we could still hear the waves washing up on the beach.

"Jacob, did you think about this? No matter where we've been today, even when we couldn't see water, we could hear breakers. I think we're on an island, but where? In the Pacific Ocean, probably off Mexico, but that doesn't help."

"I'm cold," Jacob complained. "I want to go home. I want to eat a good dinner and sleep in my own bed."

"We both want to be home, but we have to be brave until Mom and Dad come," I snapped, but then I felt bad about it. "I'm sorry. Come closer and I'll sing to you."

I looked around at the animals. Some were already asleep. In the dusk, the little white baby goats looked peaceful, like patches of moonlight on the grass. Lying there with them, I wasn't afraid of the dark like I usually am.

Then I took little Jacob in my lap to protect him. I wanted someone to hold me too, but that wasn't going to happen. I thought of our father and let one tear fall.

I was proud of our dad. He's tall, with a longish brown hair that curls around his ears. His big nose is always behind a book or behind his camera because he's a nature photographer and travels all around the world. He says he's a nerd, but he laughs about it. I can picture him clearly now, so my memory must be coming back.

I thought of our mom with her long brown hair twisted into a braid and her soft round body. She's a midwife like Grandma Jean and my Great Grandma Mira who was born at home and almost died as a newborn. This was a long time ago before they had a hospital in Liberty and she was a shoebox baby. That's what you call a very premature baby in the old days. They are so small they can fit in a shoebox. She's gone now. My mother is a nurse-midwife and she delivers babies in a hospital...

What if my parents drowned? For a second, I pictured them on the floor of the ocean tangled in seaweed and immediately locked that image in a metal box where it couldn't get out again.

It was not a cold night but it wasn't warm either and I shivered as I stared up at the stars, so beautiful, floating in the black like tiny bits of ice. *"To my little one's bedside in the night, comes a new little goat, snowy white..."* This was a song our mom used to sing. A few of the goats looked over at me and then went back to sleep, but one little white kid rose and came over. He wasn't a baby, but maybe a school age kid. I smiled as he tried to take a bite of my hair.

Then his big mother came, a black and white nanny with long droopy ears and an enormous belly. The mother goat lay down beside us, chewing a wad of sweet smelling grass and I could feel the heat from her body.

"To my little one's bedside in the night," I sang. *"Comes a new little goat, snowy white."* Jacob settled against my chest and yawned. *"The goat will trot to the market, While mother her watch does keep, To bring back raisins and almonds, Sleep little one, sleep..."*

I could almost hear our mom's low sweet voice and wished I could remember more of the song. When the little white goat snuggled up against me, I was as still as stone. Jacob's eyes closed and his breathing slowed. I pictured our mother and father and called them with my mind. **"We are here. We are alive. Come and find us."**

CHAPTER 4

DANGER

Lying next to the mother goat, I try to remember more of my life. My name is Trillium Stone and we live in West Virginia. I know that much and my brother is Jacob. Our house is white, trimmed with red and up on a hill. My dad travels a lot and when he's not home and mom has to go out for a birth, we stay with our grandparents. My best friend is Sebastian.

To the left in the grass I hear rustling and I picture a snake slithering through the grass with its little forked tongue darting in and out. When I move away, I realize again how badly I'm hurt. My face is sticky with blood, my forehead is pounding and I shudder because not only am I afraid of the dark, but the thought or sight of blood makes me sick, always has. Finally, I can't keep my burning eyes open and I fall into a dark sleep, but this time there's no dream.

Cold and stiff, just before dawn, I wake and am surprised to find that my head rests against the nanny goat's stomach. Something moves inside the animal's body and I sit straight up. The nanny's belly moves again.

The goat is pregnant! Now that I think of it, there are several nanny goats with big bellies. I lean against the stone wall behind me and look around the clearing. There are seven...eight... maybe nine or ten pregnant goats.

Jacob sleeps on, curled around the little white goat that has a black X on his face right between his eyes. Little X is his name, I decide. I'll call him Little X.

The rest of the animals are still on the ground sleeping in small groups, except King Billy, who's up on his throne on the highest rock. With strange yellow eyes, he watches me and I try to read him. He doesn't seem afraid of us, like a white tailed deer in the mountains would be. Maybe he knows we're children and doesn't feel threatened. I try to talk to him in a language he may understand, the language of the mind.

At home I have an orange cat named Willie and at certain times I can communicate with him. This is something I haven't told anyone. When we lay on my bed together and I stare into Willie's round gray-green eyes I'm sure he can understand me. Without even petting him, I can get him to purr. I can also ask him to bring his cat toy and get him to leave the room.

I lean back again, trying to blend in with the other goats. Other goats! I'm already part of the herd. Then I try an experiment. "King Billy," I call, saying the words in my mind like I do with my cat. "King Billy!"

The big goat stands up and it's hard to tell if he rises like that because he hears me or he just needs to stretch. With one leap, he jumps off his throne and thumps on the ground. Our eyes meet again and I feel his mind. There aren't any words but there's understanding. "Danger."

King Billy walks amongst the herd, touching a mother on the nose, nuzzling another. Sometimes, he stops to lick one of the babies. He has a strong odor, but the goats don't seem to mind. Maybe they're used to it. Maybe they even like it. As he comes closer the word gets louder, "Danger", and I press my back against the boulder.

The big goat's eyes are golden and shiny and his strange pupils are rectangular, not round. He stares me down and I feel how he controls the other animals, how he lets them know he's boss.

The King is telling me that he's in charge and I'd better respect him. This is his kingdom and he's in control. My brother and I are only bedding down with the herd because he allows it. With one slash of his curved white horns he could kill us.

Silently, I answer that we mean the herd no harm, that my brother and I are in trouble and alone and need his help. The great male goat blinks his yellow eyes twice. Then he turns and with a flash is back on his throne again, looking away.

DAWN

Letting out my breath, I take my sleeping brother in my arms and watch the clouds turn, first gray and then pink and then bright red. The feeling of danger is gone but I don't know if King Billy and I now have an understanding or if I just feel safer because he's up on the cliff.

As I watch the sky turn blue, I plan our day. First, we'll eat all the strange fruit we can and drink from the spring and then we have to find shelter. After that, we need better food. The fig-pears, or whatever they are, can't keep us alive forever. My stomach is already a knot of cold hunger. Also, I haven't given up on looking for a farmer or herdsman that might live nearby.

Though I hate to leave the company of the friendly goats, Jacob and I need to search further. Maybe we can find our way back to the goats again if we don't discover some people or cover by nightfall.

"Mom!" Jacob calls in his sleep. I pull his loose, damp body further into my lap. Mama Goat opens her golden eyes, shakes her black and white fur and stands up.

"Wakey, wakey, little boy," I sing. That's what our mother says when she gets us up early for school and it makes me feel sad and lost to use her words. I sing them again just like she would. "Wakey. Wakey."

Jacob opens his light brown eyes "Are we home?" he asks, looking around.

"No. We're still with the goats. After we drink some water and eat some fruit I want to look around some more. Maybe we can find some people."

"What if there aren't any people?"

"Then we'll have to live like Robinson Crusoe, until someone comes for us. Remember that story? Dad read it to us... about the man that survived alone on a desert island?"

"We could hunt," Jacob says. "I could make a spear." Though he's only eight, he's pretty smart.

"Yes, and I could make clothes out of animal skins, if there are any animals other than goats," I add. "I don't want to kill goats unless we're truly starving."

"No. They're our friends."

Little X, the white kid that had bedded down with us, is now awake and trying to eat my hair again. "Hey get off!" I laugh. Jacob laughs too and the sound of it is like bells tinkling. Soon another three goats stand up and come over. I look around the small clearing and wonder why the goats are so friendly. Have they known people before?

"Look at them," Jacob whispers. "Some of the goats have long fur and some have short. Some have droopy ears and some have ears that stand up. Their colors are all different too." He laughs again. "But they all have short stubby tails that wag like a dog's."

"And something else," I add. "Most of them have beards. See? Both male and female."

by T.S

We watch as a big male, all white in front and all black behind, struts his stiff legs and whips his short tail back and forth. He has a long beard and big dangerous curved horns and he looks up at King Billy with fierce eyes as if daring him to do anything about it.

"That's The Duke," I whisper. "He and King Billy don't like each other."

CHAPTER 5

SHELTER

ALL DAY WE WANDERED THE ROCKY LAND AND I DECIDED TO CALL IT HOPE ISLAND, BECAUSE I WAS GETTING DISCOURAGED AND I NEEDED SOME HOPE. Here and there, we found more of the pear-like fruit and one time, dark red round berries, but I wouldn't let my little brother eat them and he cried. Jacob loves berries more than anything.

"No!" I said, as I scraped them out of his hand. "They might make you sick. We have to wait to see if the goats eat them, first." For an hour he pouted, but then he forgot about it.

In the afternoon, we took a break at a high place where Jacob lay down on a boulder for a nap and I kept watch, like King Billy. From there, I could see in every direction. In front of me was only blue water and a few white seagulls sailing in the wind. No land at all, just the wide, wide sea. I scanned for airplanes or boats, but there was nothing.

Then I looked to the left. Same thing. I scooted around and looked to the right, more rocks, bushes and water. I watched a large dark bird with flat wings circle over us. An eagle, I thought, or maybe a vulture. The thought of a vulture made me shiver. Vultures ate dead things. I just hoped the big bird didn't think sleeping Jacob was dead.

Finally, I stood and searched the horizon behind me. The sun was right in my eyes and all I could see were more rocks, more small bushes and the sea, but as I gazed into the white light I spied something unusual and I stared at it for a long time. In the distance a mysterious outcrop of stone jutted above the other rocks into the sky.

"Jacob! Jacob, it's time to get going."

"No," he mumbled, his eyes shut tight. "I don't want to keep exploring."

"Wakey. Wakey." I tried our mother's singsong voice again. "Wakey. Wakey," I sang, sugary sweet. Then I shook him again, a little harder than I meant to.

"Sorry. We have to go. I saw something funny down the hill and I want to investigate."

Slowly he sat up and rubbed his face, then he moaned and tried to lie down again. Truth to tell, I was sick of him. He was holding me back. If I ditched him, I could make better time, but that wouldn't be right. We had to stick together. There could be wolves here or mountain lions. Very likely there were poisonous snakes.

Finally, I pulled Jacob up by the arm. "If we get back by dark we can take the goats some berries and see if they'll eat them. Then you can have some too." That got him going.

For hours, we wandered through the big boulders. Twice I thought I heard something in the grass, but it was probably my imagination. Some times we had to crawl over huge rocks. Sometimes we traveled through ravines so narrow we had to go sideways. I tried to keep my eyes on the towering outcrop, but I lost track of it.

As the big orange sun dropped again into the sea, I began to think I'd imagined the tower. It was our third day on Hope Island. Maybe, I was losing my mind from starvation.

It wasn't fair. Jacob and I had a home. We had parents who cared about us. Nothing like this was supposed to happen. Yet here we were, utterly alone in a strange land, apparently on an island, somewhere in the Pacific... It was like a bad dream. I pinched my arm, but I couldn't wake up.

There were tales about people who survived in the wilderness, but this was real. No one wrote about the people who didn't survive. What kind of story would that be? The wind changed and in the silence we heard a low sound.

"Water!" we said together.

Jacob scrambled off the rocks and got there first. There was a stream and the stream dropped like a little waterfall over a cliff. It was too steep to climb down, so we had to go back and find another path. By this time, the shadows were long and dark was coming.

"Dark," I thought. "It will be dark again and this time we don't even have the goats for company." We are tired; we are sunburned and starved for good food. If it were possible, I would even eat a big bowl of scrambled eggs, my least favorite food.

"Keep moving," I ordered Jacob. "I'll sing you a song. The ants go marching one by one. Hurrah. Hurrah."

"The ants go marching two by two," Jacob joined in. "Hurrah! Hurrah!"

We worked our way around an especially big rock where the stream dropped into a round pool, this time the size of a bathtub. Here we stopped to drink again and I washed my face. In the pool, I could see the shadowy reflection of a wild girl with an orange mane like a lion. There was still dried blood in my hair and I almost gagged.

I don't know why I hate blood. I just do. Someone at my new school in Liberty found out about it and now if a kid has a cut, just to be mean, he or she will pull off the bandage and show me the blood. Once a boy with skinned knees chased me around the schoolyard trying to make me sick and all the other kids laughed. That's why I didn't like our new school at first, but I'm getting used to it.

Sebastian, my friend, says, "Just tell them to bug off." He's not really a tough guy, but he can talk like one if he needs too. We're in the same class and he's smart like me. We also go to 4H Club together. 4H is an organization for children who want to learn to do real things that might help them when they grow up or help the world.

People think it's just for farm kids who want to raise sheep or chickens and enter them at the county fair, but there are six million kids in 4H and not just from farms. Sebastian and I are in a Robotics Group where we learn to make robots. It's cool.

"Look," Jacob points. "Behind the waterfall there's

a hollow. We can sleep in there." Together, we slip between the rock and the falling water and sit on the sandy floor. The heat from the day is still held in the rocks. We're hungry and tired, but now, like foxes in a den, we can curl up and sleep.

by T. S.

CHAPTER 6

GUNSHOTS

ALL NIGHT, OFF AND ON, JACOB CRIED IN HIS SLEEP. "Mama! Help!" I was sure he was reliving the nightmare of the boating accident and the hollow place in my heart grew deeper.

I held my hand in front of my face. It was so black in the rock shelter that I couldn't see my fingers and I began to imagine I was blind. If anything could be worse than being lost on an uninhabited island, it would be to be lost and blind. That would be like being in the dark forever... I was talking myself into a bad place.

Twice in the night, I thought I heard an animal drinking at the pool and I pictured a wolf. Our shelter was the size of my closet at home. If something came through the waterfall and into our hideout there was no way to get out. We were trapped.

Once a night bird cried, "Whoooooooooooo. Whoooo. Whooooooooooo. Whoooo...."

I slept, then woke, then slept again. I couldn't get

comfortable. I thought about the boy in that book called *Hatchet* that our teacher read to us back in Asheville. The kid found shelter in a cave like this, after a plane wreck. That boy was older, but he survived. I thought of Robinson Crusoe. He survived too.

I could remember things better now and I imagined our home to give myself comfort. It was a white house with red shutters on a narrow street in Liberty, West Virginia. There were flowers in the yard, zinnias and marigolds and daisies. Our mother loved flowers. And there were vegetables too, tomatoes and green peppers and broccoli. Boy, I wished I had some of those vegetables now!

I pictured our school and our town and the park along the river where we picnicked some nights when everyone was at home.

Our family didn't go to church. My Dad said that The Great Spirit was in his heart and he could worship outside and see the spirit all around him. Our mother said she talked to God every time she delivered a baby. Instead, we did lots of things together, nature stuff, like hikes and swimming and also going to historical places. I didn't know what I believed about God anyway, so I kept my mouth shut and I never asked Jacob. He was too little.

All night, in my mind, I walked around my town and

saw people and things that gave me peace, but also made me lonely. Finally, I could tell dawn was coming and the black shifted to gray. When I touched my forehead, it didn't hurt any more and I rolled on my side and considered our situation.

As far as I could tell, this rocky land seemed surrounded by water and if it was connected to a bigger piece of land, I couldn't see where. I accepted the fact that the island was probably deserted.

We'd survived three nights and I thought we could go on for a while longer, but if it got cold or another storm came, we'd be in trouble. I doubted that Jacob and I could get by forever on fig-pears and berries. People needed better food like protein. Protein was in meat, but it was also in milk and beans and nuts and eggs.

Jacob turned over and opened his eyes into the gloom. "I want to go back to the goats," he said. I supposed he'd had a dream about sleeping with the warm, kind animals. I wouldn't mind going back myself.

"Ok, lets try to find them. The cave is nice, but the goats are nicer." Just as we stood up to leave, we heard a *crack*, like the sound of a bullet. I ducked down and pulled my little brother with me.

Then, *crack*. We heard it again. Every few minutes... Crack... Crack...

Crack!...... Crack!...... Crack!

"If it's a gun, someone's a very bad hunter," Jacob whispered.

"More likely they're target practicing." I crawled outside the shelter, climbed up a high rock and keeping low on my stomach and looked all around. There was nothing to see but the same rocky landscape and the dark gray sea. "Come on, Jacob," I said quietly. "We have to investigate."

Forgetting about the mysterious rock tower, we silently reversed our path. We twisted and turned through the narrow ravines, up and down over the boulders from shadow to light, following the sounds. When the shots were very loud, we stopped. CRACK... CRACK... CRACK...

I put my hand on my little brother's shoulder, warning him to be quiet. "We don't know what the sound is, so let's sneak up like panthers," I whispered, then I motioned Jacob to follow and we climbed up another big rock. When we got to the top, I was so surprised I almost fell off the overhang.

BATTLE

Below us, the nannies and kids were backed up against the rock wall and in the center of the clearing King Billy and the Duke were fighting it out. So my instincts were right! The Duke, the big male that was white in front and black behind, was a troublemaker!

The two huge muscular animals lock their horns together, then they pull apart and King Billy rears back on his hind legs. The Duke is ready for him. He snorts and when the big white goat twists and smashes down,

their horns collide. CRACK! CRACK! CRACK! The fight goes on and I shiver.

The enraged males run backward a few yards then forward at terrific speed. Over and over they slam together, until it seems like they'll kill each other and I'm glad we're up where we can't get trampled.

Sometimes the goats stop fighting for a few minutes, while they lean against each other panting, then they start up again. The nannies are silent and the little ones tremble. The Duke has blood on his side and I try not to look at it.

Suddenly the battle is over. The Duke turns, runs away through a narrow channel in the boulders and King Billy shakes his long beard, as if to say "No big deal. Go back to what you were doing..."

Bleating follows the silence as the goats exchange comments. "Beyaa?" "Beyaaaaa?" "Beyaaaaa!"

Little X, the small white kid that shared his warmth with us two nights ago, spies our heads hanging over the ledge and climbs up to be with us. Two of the tiniest spotted brown goats begin a play-fight down below.

That night, our fourth on the island, it storms. The rain is cold and the big drops blow sideways. My brother and I go back to the hollow behind the waterfall and are surprised when Little X and his mother follow and crowd in with us. Some of the other goats come too and find shelter, here and there, in the rocks nearby.

The next morning, I wake early. In the distance the surf roars. Because I'm thirsty and want a drink of good water from the spring, I silently crawl out of the cavern. There above the pool is King Billy, lying on the top of the cliff, watching everyone. His yellow eyes meet mine, measuring me and I remember how fierce he was in the fight. This is an animal I don't need for an enemy.

"Your majesty," I whisper, bowing low, and then duck back into our den.

CHAPTER 7

THE TOWER

THE SUN WAS ALL THE WAY UP WHEN I WOKE THE SECOND TIME AND NUDGED JACOB, WHO WAS USING THE GENTLE PREGNANT NANNY FOR A PILLOW. The nanny goat opened her yellow eyes and blinked and then, as if it was an ordinary morning, Jacob stretched and ran his hand over the mother's fur.

In a flash, I remembered Jacob's bedroom. It had pale blue walls with a wallpaper border of cars and trucks. There were cars and trucks all over the floor and robots and dinosaurs, the usual things. Jacob said he was going to be a racecar driver when he grew up, but all young boys say things like that. I smiled at him, but my stomach was cold. If he grows up, I thought. Things, so far, were not looking good for us.

I could recall my bedroom too. It wasn't a pink room, like many girls have. Mine was white with orange curtains and posters of foreign countries on the walls. Mexico. Norway. China. Alaska. Our father

brought them to me from his travels as a wildlife photographer. A lump came into my throat when I remembered his twinkling brown eyes.

My eyes were hazel like Mom's, but not as kind.
Mine had a sharp glint in them, like someone who was
always thinking of a better way to do something. That
was one of my bad habits. I was too critical of others.
My Grandma Jean told me that.

There were four midwives in my family, three who
delivered babies in homes out in the country, (Grandma Jean and Great Grandma Mira and way way back,
Great-Great Grandma Patience), and then, of course,
my mother who did hospital births in town. Everyone
thought I would be a midwife too, when I grew up, and
at first I'd thought I might, because I liked babies and
it seemed a fun job.

Midwives help the mother when the babies come
out and I knew I was intelligent enough. You have to
be smart to be a midwife, have to figure things out, but
midwives also have to see blood.

Probably, I'll be a biologist instead and help save
the planet from global warming... if I survive to be
anything. Dad has been to the Arctic to take photos
and has seen the ice caps melting. He had tears in his
eyes when he told me about it... how the polar bears are
starving and dying, the beautiful white bears and their

soft white fuzzy cubs.

Everyone in our family likes to travel and we've been to all kinds of places. That's what we were doing on the ocean in the rented sailboat. I remember it now. It was my birthday trip. We flew to San Diego, California and rented a car to go camping on the beach in Baja, Mexico. I was going to be fourteen.

"Jacob," I said. "I'm so sorry. If I'd asked for a telescope or a trip to the zoo for my birthday, this disaster wouldn't have happened. Now mom and dad are gone and we're lost and it's all my fault." I didn't say everything I was thinking. Maybe our parents will never find us. Maybe they drowned. It was too awful to say.

"It's ok," Jacob said putting his arms around me "It's ok." He didn't blame me. He didn't blame anyone. He just accepted things as they were.

I don't accept things as they are! I hate bad things. I hate mean people. I hate seeing photos of sad children on TV like orphans that have no parents or refugees with no home. Now I'm one of them.

"We need food," said Jacob. That brought me out of my dark thoughts. No use feeling sorry for myself. There was work to be done. We had to find something better to eat than the fig-pears. Maybe I could steal a seagull's eggs or something. When we stood up, I noticed Mama Goat's stomach. Milk was already dripping from her udders; she must be close to having her baby.

"Let's get going, Jacob. Remember that tall straight rock in the distance, yesterday? I've been thinking that it might be a chimney. Maybe there are people here and we just haven't found them. The goats had to get here somehow."

Jacob patted the nanny on the head. "See you to-night."

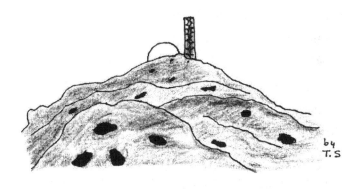

It was an hour or more into our search when Jacob tugged on the back of my shirt. "Look," he whispered pointing at a yellow flower on the ground. "A honey-bee. Where there are bees there must be honey!" Jacob had an eye for insects and he wasn't scared of them like some kids. Dad brought him preserved butterflies and even big cockroaches from around the world in small picture frames.

"I know you're hungry, but we can't think about honey. We've got to keep moving. Keep your eyes out for the rock tower."

We were almost back where we'd started when Jacob yanked on my shirt again.

"What!" The kid was irritating me with all his talk about bees and honey!

"Look." He pointed toward the sea.

"Where?" I scanned the ocean in every direction, thinking maybe he saw a boat. "Where?"

But it wasn't a boat: Jacob was shaking his finger toward the tall gray outcrop of rock outlined against the blue sky.

"Good work!" I complimented him and my little brother smiled, proud of himself for spotting it first.

"Come on." We scrambled down a boulder and traveled back along a ravine where the path twisted and turned between the huge rocks. We crossed the small stream, but this time we went further until the path seemed to end.

"Look, we can squeeze between these two boulders," Jacob said and when we did, we found ourselves in an open area, surrounded by pitted stone cliffs with deep hollows. The grass and brush were so dense it didn't look like the goats had been grazing here.

At first we didn't realize what we'd found. The

squared off tall rock at the edge of the clearing was made of many smaller rocks. It was a chimney. I was right. And the chimney was connected to a little stone cabin!

"A house," Jacob whispered. "Maybe the owners have a phone and we can call someone to come get us."

"Hello!" I yelled, a little scared. The people who lived here might not like strangers. They could be hermits or even drug dealers. Maybe that's why they built their house on this lonely island, in this remote clearing, because they were hiding from the police.

Fighting the stickers and bushes, Jacob and I crept forward until we came to an old fence made of branches woven together. Jacob pushed the gate open. This had been a yard at one time, but it was all grown up with tall weeds. We almost tripped on an old metal bucket and my heart sank as I realized the cabin was abandoned.

"No one lives here," Jacob echoed my thoughts, tears running down his little brown face.

"I guess not."

"I thought they might give us some good food and take us home. I want to see Mom. I want to see Dad." My little brother sobbed as he sank down on the stone steps. He looked so sad; I sat down with him and put my arm around his shoulders. I felt like crying too.

"It's ok, Jacob. There aren't any people here, but think of it! We've made a great discovery. If no one lives here, the house is ours!"

CHAPTER 8

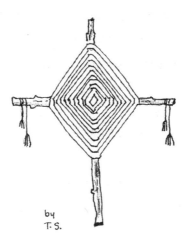

by
T. S.

THE GOD'S EYE

"HELLO," I CALLED, JUST TO BE SURE AND THEN PULLED HARD ON THE WOODEN DOOR OF THE LITTLE STONE CABIN. It creaked open. Inside, I squinted in the gloom and tried to puzzle out the story. There were books and pictures on the shelves, cooking pans hanging on nails on the beams and even some dishes left in the sink. There were clothes hanging on wooden pegs and a small cast-iron cook-stove hooked up to the stone chimney. Everything smelled old and was covered with dust.

In one corner there was a broom, a fishing pole with no line, and a walking stick. There were notebooks, a jar of pencils, a metal chest, an axe, a hammer and an old pair of leather gloves that was dusty and stiff. A straw hat hung on a peg near the door, (that would keep me from getting sunburned, I thought) and there were cobwebs all over everything.

It was a sad little one-room house that someone had once loved. I could tell this by the pictures on the walls, a mobile made of seashells that hung from the ceiling and the carvings of birds and flowers on the back of the handmade wooden chairs. There was even a huge God's eye made of driftwood and colored yarn, hanging on the wall over the hand-made wooden bed. The reds, blues and greens had faded but it was still beautiful.

A God's eye, in the shape of a cross, is something hippies and American natives made. Our Grandma Jean and Grandpa Pete had been hippies when they were young and Gram had taught me how to make a little God's eye last summer. I wiped the wetness from my eyes before Jacob could see... Our Grandma and Grandpa would love this little cabin.

While Jacob explored the cupboards along the wall, I studied the books left open on the wooden table; *Where There Is No Doctor* was the title of one. *The Homesteader's Survival Guide* was another. Bandages, gauze and an open first-aid kit were lying there too.

"Look, Jacob, this stuff on the table... I think someone must have had an accident. Maybe it was serious. Maybe they fell from the rocks or got chopped with an axe. They must have been bleeding. Maybe it was very bad. Maybe someone died." Jacob looked at me silently with big eyes then went back to his investigation on the other side of the room.

"Don't you understand? That would explain why the people left suddenly and didn't come back. They must have owned a boat." I looked around again. There were dusty and faded checked curtains at the windows and dried wild flowers in an empty jar that fell into dust when I touched them.

All day, we searched the little house for useful items and we began to feel rich. There were books on gardening and goat-keeping on the shelves. I showed them to Jacob. "That's how the goats got here. The owner of the cabin must have kept them. Maybe that's why the goats seem friendly. The old ones have been around people."

There were cookbooks and books about wild edible plants and even a few children's books. There were jackets and boots, a short piece of rope, thread and needles, a saw and even paints and brushes. All the clothes were too big, but they would be useful, at least the cloth. There was also a snakeskin under the table, but it was old and brittle and I kicked it away. That was when I saw the photo in a frame on the window ledge. "These must be the owners of the cabin," I said out loud to myself.

A dark haired man and a young blond woman, with a flower behind her ear, stood on the steps of the little stone cabin. In the picture, the grass was cut short and daisies were planted in the yard. Maybe the young woman was the one that made the curtains. Maybe the young man made the God's eye. This was their home.

"Look here!" Jacob called interrupting my thoughts. "Food." He had crawled way back into a dark lower cupboard and was pulling out tin cans and glass jars. Most of the jars were empty, but they still had lids and would be good for storing things. There were eight cans of pinto beans, three of corn, and two of peaches. There were three glass quart jars with some kind of seeds in them, perhaps wheat; two jars of oatmeal and one of brown sugar that had hardened into little rocks. There were also two bottles with corks for lids.

I opened the two bottles, both of which held yellow liquids. The first was cooking oil but it smelled terrible. The next one was vinegar and it was still good.

"It looks like the people weren't able to take very much with them," Jacob said. "They must have planned to come back."

"I wonder if the canned food is still good." I tried not to get too excited. The tin cans were old and rusty on the outside, but maybe if the food smelled ok we would try it. "Did you see any knives or a can opener?" I asked Jacob, who by now had crawled further back in the cupboards. He came out, grinning, with one more prize, the best one of all, a big jar of wooden matches and seven candles. Fire! I thought. We have fire! We have light! We won't have to be in the dark at night.

Jacob found a sharp hunting knife and I pried open a can of beans, then we collected a few dry sticks and I made a small fire in the cook stove. After boiling the canned beans for a long time we ate them and they were great! For the first time in days, we weren't hungry.

How to Make a Fire in a Wood Cook Stove

First collect a pile of small twigs and branches.

Then take a few pieces of paper from a stack of old newspapers.

(If you don't have paper you can use dried leaves or dried grass.)

Crumple them in the metal firebox on the side of the stove.

Lay small twigs, called kindling, on top of the paper.

Next open the damper if there is one in the chimney.

This is a little device that keeps the fire from burning too hot.

If you don't open the damper you will get smoke in your cabin.

Carefully strike a match, light the flame

and blow on it to get it to spread.

Once the kindling is burning, add bigger sticks.

CHAPTER 9

A SCREAM IN THE NIGHT

"IN A CABIN IN THE WOODS. A LITTLE OLD MAN BY THE WINDOW STOOD," I SANG TO MY BROTHER. It was a silly 4H Camp song, but I sang it soft and slow like a lullaby. Jacob was snuggled against me on a bed for the first time since we were shipwrecked.

In a metal chest in the corner, I'd found a green quilt, two old pillows and two sheets. They smelled dusty but they would do and we could hang them out to air in the morning.

At sunset, I covered the mattress and made a nice nest for the two of us. Before it got dark, I brought water in a bucket from the pool in the rocks and even made Jacob wash his face and hands. There was a sink, but no plumbing and I discovered that the wastewater flowed into a bucket that would have to be dumped outside when it got full.

I bolted the heavy handmade door with the wooden bolt. I didn't know if there were any people or wild animals on Hope Island, but it still made me feel safer. After we crawled in bed I lay looking at my brother as he slept, his face in a patch of moonlight that came from the window.

Some people might think it was strange to have a brother and sister of two different colors, one brown and one white with freckles, but humans come in all colors just like the goats. Why not?

When we first moved to Liberty some of the kids at school said bad things to my brother, because of his race, but I told the principal and he said he'd take care of it. Mr. Davis is brown skinned too and used to play on the Torrington State University football team. Nobody messes with Mr. Davis.

I lay and looked up at the wooden beams and the wooden ceiling. Someone had spent a long time building this cabin and the rock walls of our new home would keep out the weather. Two small windows let in the moonlight. It was like camping, only better. Except for the cold in my heart when I thought of our family, I could almost be happy.

Where was our family now? Were they out on the ocean with a search party? I tried to send them a picture of Hope Island and the little stone house, but I didn't know where the island was located or how to describe it.

For now, Jacob was all the family I had. My Gram said a family could be any size or any kind of people, a Father and a son, or two mothers and two little girls or maybe just a single person and their pets, or even a bunch of people who weren't related, but lived together and took care of each other. Right now it was just Jacob and me.

In the middle of the night I sat straight up in bed, my heart pounding. The moon had gone down and the room was pitch black. For a moment I didn't know where I was. It was a scream that woke me and I couldn't tell if it was a nightmare or real. I waited. The room was blacker than an underground cave. Jacob was sitting up too.

"Did you hear that?" he whispered.

I nodded. "What was it?"

"It sounded like a lady or a girl." Jacob slipped out of bed, pulled a chair over to one of the windows and climbed up on it.

Then the sound came again. "AIEEEEEEEEEE!" And it made the hair stand up on my neck.

"Someone's in trouble." That was Jacob. I felt around for the jar of matches, lit a candle and stuck it in the little handmade tin lantern.

We looked at each other. "What should we do?" I asked.

"If mom and dad were here, they would go help." Jacob jumped off the chair and pulled on his pants. He put on his shoes and started for the door without even tying them. I really didn't want to go. There might be creatures out in the dark. I remembered hearing something drinking in the pool by the waterfall... and I knew there were snakes. I'd seen the snakeskin...

MOTHER GOAT

The sound came again and again. Jacob unbolted the door.

"No wait! I'm coming too," I couldn't let him go alone. Yanking on my shorts, I stepped into my shoes. I lighted a candle, put it in the tin lantern and grabbed the axe. If we needed a weapon, at least we would have one.

Back through the thicket of overgrown brush we hurried, heading for the sound of the screams. It was hard going with just a flickering candle for light. Then a branch hit me in the face. "Sugar!" I swore. "Wait, Jacob!" He was running ahead.

"Over here," Jacob hissed. "The cries are coming from inside the rocks." We made the turn at the narrow place between the big boulders near the waterfall and were surprised to find the black and white mother goat lying on her side. It was hard to see, but she appeared to be straining and something was sticking out of her backside.

"It's Mother Goat trying to have her baby, but something's not right. Look there's just one little hoof sticking out. Remember when we saw the kittens born at Grandma's? She said the head's suppose to come first."

"I remember," Jacob nodded, squatting down and petting the mother goat with one hand. "Shhh. Shhh. Shhh," he said.

by T. S.

"There's a book about goats on the shelves in the cabin. Maybe we can figure out how to help her. I'll run back. Can you stay here?"

I didn't know if it was right to leave an eight year old sitting alone in the dark in this wild place, but it didn't seem right to leave Mother Goat by herself either. She seemed to be in so much pain and so scared.

Every few minutes she would hump up her back and cry, "EEYAAAAAA!" She was pushing but nothing was happening. The baby was stuck. It was a horrible sound. So pitiful it made my toes curl.

"I'll stay," Jacob answered, stroking the nanny goat's head. He wasn't afraid. Between pains, Mother Goat would lick his hand.

Leaving the axe and the lantern with my brother, I dashed back through the bushes. At first I was worried I wouldn't find the little stone building in the dark, but then I saw the gleam of the window glass when the moon came out of the clouds.

Inside, I found another candle, lit it and reached up on the shelf for the worn copy of *Goats: A Guide to Their Care.* Quickly, I flipped to a section calling "Kidding." (Since baby goats are called kids, I decided that might be the chapter that would tell how to help a nanny goat give birth to her baby.)

"EEYAAAAAA!" I heard in the distance and I stuck the book under my arm and hurried back to the spring.

"EEYAAAAAA!" the crying got louder.

Then the sound stopped. By the time I found Jacob and Mother Goat, a baby had been born, but it was dead. My little brother was holding the limp wet animal in his lap and tears ran down his face.

"It came out, but it didn't breathe," he choked out.

I reached over and took the limp animal, not even thinking about the blood or the goo. I just wanted to save the baby. I remembered how on TV a doctor breathes for the patient and brings him back to life. Puff, puff, puff, I tried blowing into the little animal's mouth, but it was no good.

Mother Goat twisted around to see what was happening, so we gently laid the dead baby next to her. The tiny white and black spotted goat looked perfect, but it had been coming out wrong for too long. Mother Goat licked its face. "Bleeeeeeeeeeh," she said sadly. Then she stood up and got a drink of water.

"Should we take it home?" Jacob asked.

"I guess so. For sure, we shouldn't leave the dead body by the pool of good water." So, I carried the little kid in my arms back to the stone house and placed it on the ground. Mother Goat followed and lay next to it with a sigh.

CHAPTER **10**

A CUP OF MILK

IN THE MORNING, I HAD AN IDEA. Mother Goat still stood outside by her dead baby, sadly munching the tall grass. I opened the goat book to the chapter on milking, read what it said and looked at the pictures. Then I found a tin cooking pot and washed it out good.

"Here, Jacob. Help me. Take this piece of rope and tie Mother Goat to the fence. I'm going to milk her. I once tried milking a cow with Grandpa Pete, but it was too hard and I gave it up. This time we really need the milk and there's no Grandpa to help us, so I'll try harder." Squish, I pulled down on one of the udders.

Mother Goat didn't move. She almost seemed happy to be milked. Her bag was so full and tight and she had no baby to nurse. Splash went the warm white liquid into the pan. Squish, I pulled on the other udder. It was working! Squish-Splash. Squish-Splash. Squish-Splash. Then I tried using both hands. "Look Jacob! Milk."

When my fingers got tired and I stopped for a break, Jacob wanted to try. "I can do it too," he said, but it was harder than it looked. At first he couldn't get any milk; his hands were too little, but then he got the hang of it. Squish-Splash. Squish-Splash. Squish-Splash.

In the end we had enough for two cups. Goat's milk didn't taste like cold milk out of the fridge. It wasn't even the same as warm milk from Grandpa's cows, but we were so hungry we didn't care. It was delicious.

That morning, for breakfast, we cooked and ate oatmeal, with some of the hard brown sugar and the warm goat's milk. Afterwards, we took a rusty shovel we found leaning against the side of the cabin and buried the baby goat in the clearing. We laid a flat rock on it for a tombstone and I said a few words.

"Dear baby goat. I'm sorry we couldn't save you. I promise I will read the book and know more what to do if another mother goat has trouble. Rest in Peace." Mother Goat munched some grass. It was like she had already forgotten, but we didn't forget.

HOW TO MILK A GOAT OR COW

If you are ever starving, here's how to milk a goat or cow.
Grab the teat between your point finger and thumb
as high as you can.
Squish firmly to push the milk down into the teat.
Now here's the hard part.
While keeping your thumb and first finger tight,
bring your palm and other fingers together.
This will make the milk squirt out.
If you don't get any, keep trying.
It's because you aren't keeping your thumb and first finger
pinched hard enough.
Good Luck.

SETTLING IN

In the days that followed the death of the baby goat, we organized the cabin. It was hard for two children who hadn't done much real work before, but since we didn't know when we'd be rescued, we wanted to make our lives as comfortable and safe as possible.

First we cleaned. There were spider webs and spiders. There was dust and mice poop. It was a real mess. While we were cleaning, we discovered more useful items, a backpack, an old tent, a canteen, a coffee can full of nails, a jar of soap and a pair of scissors.

One day ran into the next. Every morning we went up to the cliffs and looked down at the ocean, hoping to see a boat, but the waves just rolled in and we never saw one. Every afternoon we worked on the cabin. We took everything off the narrow bookshelves, wiped them and put the books back again.

The book about goats interested me most and I took a few minutes to look through the pages. Here's what I learned. Goats are very social. They were the first animals to be used by man and the first animals to be milked. Most goats can be found in Asia and the Middle East. There are over 210 breeds and around 450

by T. S.

million tamed goats around the world. Some breeds of goats always get pregnant in the fall and some can get pregnant any old time. Goats first came to the New World with Christopher Columbus, in 1492.

There were also a few children's books on the big bookshelf. "Look, Jacob. Some of our favorites... *Charlotte's Web* and *The Little House on the Prairie*, *The Indian in the Cupboard* and *Call of the Wild*."

There was a paperback that caught my eye, *Living on the Earth*. I couldn't tell if it was a picture book for kids or grown-ups but it had lots of drawings. I liked to draw and I'm a pretty good artist, if I say so myself. I thumbed through the book and saw it had pictures of hippies living a natural life and directions for how to make things. That made me smile. One of the women wore a long skirt and looked like our Grandma Jean when she was young. I put that one aside for later and went on cleaning.

"I miss mom. I miss dad. I miss my matchbox cars and action men. I miss TV. I miss ice cream... There's nothing to do here... I'm bored." Jacob complained.

"Quit it, would you!" I yelled. "And get back to work or shut up." Then I felt bad about it. Jacob had actually helped a lot. While he was playing outside in the clearing, he discovered a recess in the rocks that contained garden tools, shovels, rakes and a curved knife with a wooden handle to cut brush. There were empty buckets and a few boards that were smoothed by the waves. I put him in charge of the tools and we called the cavern the shed.

All those things could be useful, if we had to stay on the island for a long time. I didn't like that thought, but I remembered something Grandma Jean used to say. "Prepare for the worst, but hope for the best." Prepare for the worst, but hope for the best. That's what we were going to do.

BLOOD

One day, as we were cutting down the tall grass and brush behind the cabin, we found an old outhouse with a white toilet seat and a lid. It was about the size of a small shower stall and someone had carved a moon in the door.

Before that we had to go to the bathroom in the tall grass. We still didn't have any toilet paper, but we used pieces of old newspaper from the cabin, so that wasn't too bad. It's funny how just having an outhouse made our life seem more comfortable.

While chopping brush with the long curved knife, Jacob stared down at his leg. "Ow!" he said under his breath, but he didn't stop working. "Look, Trillium, a fire pit made of stone with a metal grill." He was excited and I was too, until I saw the blood running down his shin.

"Oh, no! You're bleeding!" I wanted to run away because of the blood, but the gash needed attention. Old rusty things that cut your skin can give you infection. I knew about this because once when I was nine I'd stepped on a nail and my mom told me I had to go to the hospital for a tetanus shot. I didn't know what tetanus was and I cried, but my mother, who was a nurse and a midwife, told me I had to go. "No argument! No question!"

"You can die from bacteria off rusted metal," she explained, but still I didn't want to go. I hated shots and I hid in the playhouse until my dad found me and carried me, still screaming, out to the car. Now Jacob was cut, there was no mom or dad and no hospital and no tetanus shot, so I had to fix him or he might die. This was serious.

I trudged into the cabin. "You've got to be more careful, Jacob! Now I have to clean your cut and wrap it." I sounded angry, but really I was just scared. There was nothing I hated more than blood, except maybe the dark... and being alone on an island.

"It's ok," Jacob said. "It doesn't hurt." He was still struggling to pull the grill out of the grass.

"I mean now. You have to come inside and we have to clean it right now!" Jacob walked slowly inside.

"If the soap stings, use your childbirth breathing." This was something we'd learned from our mother as way of making pain easier when a woman is having a baby, but it works for any kind of pain. "Here's what you do," I reminded my brother. "Go, hee, hee... whoo, whoo. The whoo whoo is like blowing out a candle."

I got a clean basin and lots of clean water. Then I took soap and washed the cut good. Twice I gagged and almost threw up, but I kept going as the water in the basin turned pink and then red. I scrubbed the cut and dried it, then I got down the old first aid kit, put ointment on and tied bandages around Jacob's leg. Finally I gave my brother a pillow and even though he didn't want to, I made him lie down.

"I'm sorry I cut myself and you had to clean it for me. I always mess things up," he apologized.

"Don't say that. You found the fire ring and the grate. Now when it's hot, we can cook outside. And you were brave about letting me take care of you. The fact is we were both brave. You didn't cry at all and I made it through without losing my breakfast!"

CHAPTER 11

by Trillium

PLAYING HOUSE

FOR THE NEXT FEW DAYS, BECAUSE WE NEEDED THE MILK, WE KEPT MAMA GOAT TIED UP. Finally, when she was used to us, we let her go free to graze with the other goats. That night we waited, afraid she wouldn't come back, but she did and she brought little X with her and a few other kids that were old enough to be away from their mothers.

The next night, a few of the other nannies followed Mother Goat to the clearing. She seemed to be their leader. Each day more showed up, until the whole herd bedded down in the meadow at night. Even King Billy came and stayed up on the high rocks, watching.

When we first arrived on Hope Island, I noticed that many of the goats looked pregnant. Sure enough, every few days, another nanny would start acting strange. For a few hours she would disappear and then come back licking a tiny newborn kid. Most of them gave birth without any problems, even when they had twins.

Grandma Jean, who'd delivered hundreds of babies, maybe thousands, including me, said that most animals could give birth alone if they had to, even people, but it was nice to have someone around... just in case.

One morning, on my way out to milk Mother Goat, I stopped on the cottage's stone steps. Because the goats were grazing, the clearing was starting to look like a park surrounded by gray-pitted cliffs. With the tall grass and thick brush gone, you could see that many of the big boulders had deep hollows in them, like the little cave behind the waterfall and the cave where the tools were stored. I imagined that the homesteaders had kept their goats in the hollows at night or when the weather was bad.

I now thought of the people who'd lived in the cabin as "the homesteaders." Homesteaders, I'd learned in school, were pioneers in the old days, who built their houses in the wilderness, but there were modern homesteaders too, people who wanted to live a simple life, away from the hustle and bustle and pollution of cities.

I used to think that sounded cool, to go back to the land and live in the wilderness, but now that we were actually doing it, I wasn't so sure. It was a lot of work and I missed the easy ways of doing things, like micro-waves and washing machines, refrigerators and com-puters.

In the afternoon, I got out some of the homestead-er's old clothes and cut down the legs and arms so that Jacob and I could wear them. When we put them on, we burst out laughing because we looked like clowns, but we didn't care. There was no one to see us.

We needed to do a wash, so I found a big tub out back and carried five buckets of water from the water-fall. Back and forth I went, until my arms ached. Then I had to build a fire in the fire pit and heat the water in the tub. Finally, Jacob and I had to move the tub to the steps. This was the most dangerous, because the hot wa-ter could burn us if it spilled. Finally, I had to scrub the clothes and the sheets on the washboard, an old-fash-ioned metal gadget that I'd only seen in cowboy movies.

When I was done, we hauled more water, but this time we didn't heat it. I rinsed the laundry in cold and hung it on a rope that we tied from the cabin to the out-house.

All the time I worked, I sang like I was a cheerful pioneer woman. "She'll be coming around the mountain when she comes. She'll be coming around the mountain when she comes..."

We were playing house, playing homesteaders. It was just a game, until we were rescued.

A HAPPY DAY

Life was gradually improving for us and I started to think we might make it. We had milk twice a day. We had the strange fig-pears. We were even eating some wild edible greens that I found down by the spring. The dark green plants grew all around the pool and were called watercress. I recognized the plant because our mom had bought some at the grocery store. It was spicy and good.

"You look funny wearing those baggy old clothes," Jacob teased. "I hope you don't wear them to school." It was a good joke since there was no school on the island and no one to see us. It did make me think though... about clothes and what a big deal they were when I lived back in Liberty. Now I knew that when it comes down to staying alive, none of that matters.

Above us, big white clouds sailed across the blue sky. Seagulls flew over and sometimes a vulture or maybe an eagle, but it was nice sitting on the warm stone porch.

"Listen!" Jacob said. "Do you hear that?"

"What?"

"BEYAAAA!"

"It's a pregnant goat!" Jacob shouted. "Just like the other time."

We heard it again. "EYAAAAAA!" It sounded like Mama Goat when she was in trouble. Every few minutes the cry repeated.

This time I was prepared. Like our Grandma Jean who did home births, we now had a "birth kit." In the cloth bag, I'd collected some supplies I'd read about in the goat book; soap, a piece of thick twine about four feet long, in case a baby got stuck, clean rags to dry the baby goat with and a candle and matches if we had to go out at night.

"Come on," Jacob yelled as he slammed out the door. I grabbed the bag and ran after him to a narrow shady place between two boulders. There, we found a small black nanny with a very round stomach lying on her side. Her eyes were big and you could tell she was frightened.

"Maybe it's her first baby," Jacob whispered. "It's

ok. It's ok," he moved toward her slowly with his hand out and the nanny licked it. Then she strained and a speckled balloon pushed out of her backside.

"What's that?" Jacob wondered. "That doesn't look right."

"It's the water bag. Human babies have them too. Sometimes doctors pop them, but Mom said mid-wives try not to. It will pop by itself." Just then water splashed everywhere. I was ready for it and jumped back, but Jacob got his sneakers wet.

"Feel better, Midnight?" he asked. The all black goat didn't have a name before, but she did now. Mid-night.

"EEEYAAAAA!" Midnight humped up again and it seemed to me that she must be new at this. Nothing was really wrong. The baby's head and both the front hooves were coming out, just like the picture in the goat book.

"It's ok," said Jacob in his soft voice. "It's ok." The nanny looked at him with her yellow eyes.

"You can do it. Push!" we encouraged her and I couldn't help tightening my stomach muscles, bearing down for the mother. "BEYAAAAAAAAA!" the small nanny said and stood up, stomping her feet as the body of the baby inched its way forward.

Jacob kept his hand on the goat's back patting her.

I wanted to pull the kid out, it made me so nervous just watching, but I knew from the goat book that, unless you thought the baby might die, you should let the mother do it on her own. It's the same with humans, my mom said. Keep your hands off unless the mother or baby need you.

Already we could see that this little goat would be ok. He wrinkled up his face and sneezed even before he was born. Midnight lay down and gave one more big push and the whole body slid out.

Finally, I could do something. I was ready with my towel to wipe the newborn off, but Jacob held out his hand to stop me.

"Look," he said. "The mother goat is already doing it."

"Beyaaaa," she said softly, licking her baby and looking surprised and happy.

The little goat squirmed closer to his mother. "Bleeee," he answered and then sneezed again.

But the birth wasn't over yet. Something else was coming. Part of the water bag was hanging out of the Goat's bottom and it was slimy and covered with blood. "Yuck!" I gagged when the nanny pushed again and the mess plopped on the ground.

Jacob shoved it away with a stick, where I couldn't see it, because he knew how I hated blood. Then we both laughed as the sun streamed through ravine, onto the mother and baby. The little goat searched for his Mama's teat and found what he was looking for. It was one happy day.

CHAPTER **12**

THE JUNGLE GYM

The more the goats grazed in the meadow, the prettier it got, until the animals had eaten most of the thorn bushes and tall weeds and there was just short grass.

In the middle of the clearing, a big dead pine tree, with many twisty limbs, served as jungle gym for the young goats and sometimes when Jacob and I were tired and had finished our chores, we lay in the grass nearby and watched them play.

"Did you know goats could climb trees," my brother asked me one day.

"Are you kidding? I never would have imagined it! Little X and his friends jump from limb to limb and even chase each other. There is no point in doing it, except to have fun. People and goats aren't so different. Everyone likes to have fun."

"Look," Jacob rolled over. "It's another bee. I know there's got to be honey somewhere around here. Hey, there's another." I watched as he crawled through the grass on his hands and knees.

"Be careful, Jacob. If you don't watch out, you're going to get stung!" As usual Jacob didn't pay any attention and I halfway wished he would get stung, just to make my point. He was standing now, shading his eyes and looking up at the rocks.

"See the low point in the cliff? They're all flying toward it," he whispered, as if the insects would know he was on to them. "When bees have pollen they head for their hive. Let's follow them."

I looked across the clearing. The shadows were long and the sun was low in the sky. It wasn't a good time to go exploring, so I pulled him down and tickled him to get his mind off the bees.

Jacob was small for his age and irritating sometimes, even lazy in my opinion, but I had to admit, he knew more than most kids. He wouldn't forget about the bees. He'd keep working it out, but I'd have to watch him or he'd go wandering off to find the hive by himself.

"You are my honey!" I said as I pulled his shirt up and gave him a buzz on his stomach.

HUNGER

The first thing every morning, when I woke up, I thought about food. After breakfast I thought about what we would eat for lunch. And after lunch I planned what we could have for dinner.

There were no snacks in between. There was no refrigerator to raid. There was no store where we could buy treats. Often, we had so little we had to go to bed hungry. On those nights, I dreamed of donuts and cookies, pies and cakes, things we couldn't have.

The sugar we'd found in the glass jar was gone and so were the dried beans and all the canned food. All we had was the milk, fig-pears, and the three jars of wheat, but I didn't know what to do with them.

In the evenings, I studied the books about collecting wild plants and in the day, we followed the goats to see what they ate. Already, we'd tried some edible plants.

We cooked dandelion leaves, which tasted like spinach and we ate sorrel raw because it tasted like lemons. I learned their names from comparing the shape of the leaves to the drawings in a well-worn copy of the home-steader's book called *Stalking the Wild Asparagus*.

We picked berries too, but we watched the goats eat them first. The dark red ones were sweet and good. I even dried some on an old window screen I found leaning against the house. The book said you could save fruit that way and I was beginning to think our stay on Hope Island might last another few weeks.

The feeling of hunger is something I'd never felt before. Not really. I said I was hungry back home in Liberty, but that wasn't real hunger. Real hunger is painful, like the stomach trying to eat itself.

To keep track of the days, I made notches with a hunting knife on the walking stick in the cabin. It

by Trillium

now had seventeen cuts. Had it really been that long? We'd been working so hard, I hadn't noticed. One day ran into the next, marked only by the sunrise and our will to survive.

Morning and evening, both Mama Goat and Midnight, waited by the house to be milked. Midnight had her baby to nurse, but she had more than enough extra milk and she seemed to like the attention. We stored the wonderful white liquid in clean glass jars in the spring to keep cold.

When I thought about those first few days on the island, when we only had the pear-figs and water, I was determined to have food on hand always... always to be prepared. It was an obsession.

Every morning, while I investigated the books in the cabin, Jacob practiced spelling words and math problems that I'd copied into one of the homesteader's notebooks. I didn't want him to be too far behind when we got back to school.

I also showed him how to do things that most eight year olds wouldn't be allowed to do. He could light matches and build a fire, but only if I was present. Fire was scary and if the wooden parts of the cabin burned down we'd be in deep trouble. I also showed him how to cook figs and wild greens. I taught him these things, in case anything happened to me. Like Grandma said, prepare for the worst and hope for the best.

In the afternoon, when we were done with our work, I let my little brother play. He drew pictures of cars and trucks on smooth flat white rocks that he kept in an old tin can. "Vrooom!" "Beep. Beep," he made the sounds as he rammed them together in a crash.

Then he sang, "We-oooo. We-ooo." That was the ambulance coming. It made me smile to see him having fun. I would do the worrying.

One day, I threw the books down. We'd been working so hard, cleaning up the cabin and gathering wild greens and fruit and wood to cook the food, that it had been days since we'd taken time to explore more of the island. "I'm tired of this. Let's go back down to the beach."

"Ok, I can collect some more flat stones," Jacob, said. "I'm going to make a train."

It was amazing how the little guy could entertain himself.

CHAPTER 13

T.S

A SERIOUS ERROR

Soon my brother and I were at the top of the bluff. Four young goats had followed us, trailing along like dogs, but they stopped at the edge. They knew if they went down, they'd have to climb up again.

I was surprised how suddenly the island dropped off and I stood with my hands on my hips staring down at the white sand of a cove that we'd never seen before. It was a perfect half circle and the waves weren't so rough.

"Why hasn't anyone come for us?" I thought out loud and then wished I'd kept my mouth shut.

"They're searching, aren't they?" Jacob asked, looking worried.

"Of course, but we've been working so hard to make a home and find food that I hadn't thought that a boat or an airplane could pass by and not even know we were here. Dumb! Dumb! What was I thinking? That our parents would just come strolling into the clearing one day or a helicopter would fly over and see us? The ocean is huge. This is one tiny island..." Jacob looked really scared now.

"The first few days, I was just in a panic and then my head injury must have affected me more than I thought. It was probably a concussion like football players get. After we found the cabin I was concentrating on making it clean and safe and getting food, just trying to survive. We should have set up a signal of some sort right away."

"I just thought they'd figure out where we were." Jacob said, but he was just a little kid.

I turned my head so Jacob couldn't see my tears. "No, I should have known better." What I didn't say was... Now maybe the search and rescue people have already passed. "Dumb! Dumb!"

"Stop beating yourself up," Jacob said, sounding just like our father. "What you need to do is learn from your mistakes."

Tomorrow... I thought. Tomorrow we will have to make some sort of signal flags to put up on the sea cliffs.

FISH TRAP

Down on the shore, we found ourselves on a white beach shaped like a crescent moon.

"Look, Trillium! A dead fish."

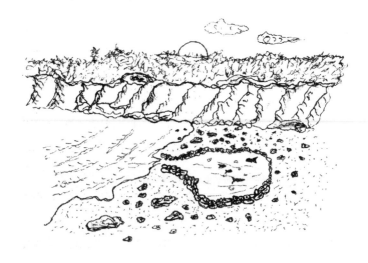

"Gross!" I wrinkled my nose. The fish was rotten and flies were all over it.

"We could catch one of these, if we had a hook for our fishing pole," my brother thought out loud.

"Maybe we don't need one," I said. "Yesterday, I saw a picture in the survival manual that showed how to build a fish trap out of rocks. We have to find a low place where the tide will come in." I looked around. "You can stay here, but don't go in the water over your knees. I'm going to check it out."

Wandering down the shoreline, I noticed pretty seashells sparkling in the sand. Before we were shipwrecked, I would have collected them, but now such things didn't interest me. All I could think of was food.

On the side of a huge gray rock I caught sight of a lizard about ten inches long. He turned his head and stared at me with his beady red eyes and then disappeared down a crack. We could kill a lizard and roast it over a fire, I thought, but I wasn't that hungry and hoped I never would be.

As I searched the beach for a low place, I watched sea gulls swoop like white kites through the air and little sea birds run in front of me and peck in the sand. Finally, I found a low place where the big rocks came down to the water.

All I'd have to do was pile up smaller stones about

two feet high. When the tide was high and the water was up, fish would swim in and when the tide went out and the water was low, the fish would be trapped. I began work at once and was so involved in hauling the rocks that I didn't notice the sun was so low.

How to Build a Fish Trap on the Beach Without Any Tools

If you ever need to get fish for food
and don't have a fishing pole or a hook,
find a place on the beach where there are plenty of rocks.
Arrange the rocks in a U shape about two feet high
with the wide part of the U facing out toward the water.
At the opening, make a row of lower rocks
so that when the tide is high the fish will swim in
and when the tide is low they'll get stuck in the trap.
You'll also need a spear made of straight wood with a sharp point,
or a net if you can find one.

CHAPTER 14

GOLDEN EAGLE

As I WORKED A WORD CAME INTO MY HEAD. "Danger." It was almost like I'd heard it out loud.

"Jacob!" I called heading back where I'd left him. "Jacob!" It would soon be dark and I wanted to get home. "JACOB!" My voice echoed off the gray-pitted stone, but there was no answer

"Just like the little kid to go wandering off," I mumbled. I was mad at my brother, but I was mad at myself too. After almost drowning in the dark cold water, you'd think I'd be more afraid of the ocean. I'd gotten carried away trying to build a fish trap and now where was he? Maybe he went back to the cabin.

I began to scurry up the cliff, pulling myself over the rocks. Twice I almost fell. At the highest point I was surprised to meet King Billy. He was standing on a ledge looking inland.

"Have you seen my brother?" I asked knowing The King couldn't answer. He looked at me sideways with his strange golden eyes and then looked again in the direction of the clearing. I swallowed hard. I was worried.

"What if Jacob walked too far out?" I wondered out loud. "What if a big wave came and knocked him off his feet and swept him out where the water is dark and deep? What if a shark came close to the beach and grabbed him?"

King Billy sniffed the air and shook his long white coat. The word came into my head again, loud and clear this time, "DANGER." The King pawed the ground. Then he took off. There was trouble. I was sure of it.

Leaping from boulder to boulder, the big goat dashed ahead of me. I followed as best I could, but he was more sure-footed and he knew the trails. Down into the ravines he galloped, then twisted and turned through the narrow paths and into the clearing around the stone house.

"Jacob!" I was panting so hard I could barely speak and I had a pain in my left side from running. "Jacob!" but there was no answer. On the far side of the meadow, I could hear goats bleating. "That's where my brother must be," I gasped.

King Billy was headed that way, so I ran with him. Showers of pebbles shot out behind as he scrambled up the boulders and at the crest I saw what was causing the trouble. A golden eagle was soaring above a group of small kids, Little X and his pals.

"Beyaaaaaa" cried the young goats and there was Jacob right in the middle of them!

The eagle circled, getting lower each time, its wings stretched wide. As the sun slipped into the ocean and turned the sky orange, I could see each golden feather.

I knew that the eagle needed food, maybe she even had baby eagles to feed back at her nest. She was part of the circle of life, but she didn't need to eat my goats or my little brother! The eagle could go to another island, or eat figs and fish...

Then the big bird dropped. Straight down she came with her sharp curved claws stretched out in front of her.

"Nooooo!" I yelled, but I couldn't run fast enough to get to Jacob in time. King Billy was trying. He leapt across the flat tops of the high rocks.

Jacob saw the eagle plunging, but there was no-where to hide so he crouched against a boulder and put his hands over his head. He looked so little like that. The eagle would try for the smallest creature.

"NOOOO!" I screamed again. "Stand up Jacob. Make your self BIG. Wave your arms around."

For once he did what I said. Climbing up on the bolder, he stared right at the diving bird, roared like a lion and whirled his arms around like a windmill. The eagle made another turn to gather speed.

"AURRRGGGG! AURRRGGGG! AURRRGG-GG!" Jacob roared.

King Billy was still too far away to help. "BE-Yeaaaaahhhhhhh!" called the goats.

Just then, up through a ravine, came another male goat, white in front, and black behind. It was The Duke! He jumped up on his hind legs, the same way he did when he fought King Billy and struck out at the huge bird. They collided, then the golden eagle swerved and dropped away to the sea.

My heart was pounding like a drum, I couldn't catch my breath and I sat down sobbing. Sometimes Jacob was lazy. He didn't mind me, but I loved him with all my heart and if anything happened to him...

Now he ran over. "Did you see me, Trill? Did you see? I did what you said and I chased the eagle away.

I saved the goats. The Duke and I together, we saved them." Then he saw my tears and put his arms around me. Even though I was bigger, he held me close. "It's ok," he told me. "It's ok."

Across the way, the goats were bleating again. King Billy had just arrived and the Duke was leaving with blood on his eye where the eagle had clawed him. The King followed. Was there going to be another battle with crashing horns?

No. King Billy stepped up to the Duke and bowed his head as if thanking him. The Duke bowed back. Their horns clicked and they touched noses as if they were friends.

FISH AND FLAGS

The very next day, I woke thinking about flags. We were spending all our time getting food and fixing up the cabin, but I didn't want to stay on Hope Island forever.

The event with the eagle had terrified me. We were just kids. Someday something serious could happen to either of us. We could get sick or injured and then what? We needed a signal, something that could be seen by air or water. That's where the flags came in. First thing after breakfast, I began to search the cabin.

"What are you looking for?" Jacob asked finishing his bowl of cooked figs and goat's milk.

"Cloth. We're going to make some signal flags to put up on the high rocks, I just don't want to tear up anything useful."

"What about the old tent under the bed," he suggested. "We could cut up the canvas. It's has lots of holes and isn't much good for anything." So that's what we did.

First we spread the tent on the floor, so we could use the scissors to cut six squares of cloth. Then I pried the lid off an old can of red paint.

"Darn! It's all dried up."

"Put some water in it," Jacob suggested and it worked. When I put hot water in the can and stirred it with the hunting knife, it became paint again. Next, we took the old paint-brushes and painted the word HELP on every square. Finally we nailed the flags on long poles.

By afternoon, we'd arranged all our signals on every high point around the island by jamming the poles into cracks in the rocks. I stood back and was satisfied. That was all I could think of to do, so we went down to finish the fish trap to see if we'd caught anything.

"What were you doing up on the cliff with the baby goats when the eagle attacked you?" I asked as we climbed down the cliff. "You could have been killed. I was so scared. You were supposed to stay with me."

"I was tracking the bees. Each time I see one they're headed in the same direction. It's called a beeline and it will lead to their honey. I'm sorry I scared you... I was scared too. I thought the eagle was going to get me. But did you see? Did you see me do it? Arghhhhhh-hh!" he yelled and whirled his arms around like before. "Arghhhhhhhh!" He looked so funny I had to laugh.

"Do you think it will work?" Jacob changed the subject, looking up at the signal flags that flapped in the wind. I tightened my mouth.

"I hope so..."

For the next few days, when we went to check the flags, we also went down to inspect the fish trap. I made my little brother come, because I couldn't trust him alone anymore. He might wander off. Each time we had to fool around with the rocks, because they were either too high or too low.

If they were too high the fish couldn't get in when the tide was up. If they were too low, the fish would all swim away when the tide went down. At first Jacob helped by carrying more stones, but after awhile he just played in the water.

Finally, one afternoon, he stuck out his chin and refused to come with me. He was lying on the floor messing around with the train he had made from his new white stones.

"You've got to come!" I yelled. "I can't trust you alone."

"You're not my boss," he yelled back. "Anyway, it takes too long and we never get any fish. I'm going to stay here and play."

Great! What was I going to do? I couldn't spank him. I was stronger and could probably tie him up, but that would seem wrong. I stared down at him. His little brown legs and arms were getting skinny. His frizzy dark hair was tangled. His face was dirty and he needed a bath. Jacob looked like a wild boy and I was fed up.

It was more work to drag him along than let him stay here. If he wanted to wander away and get eaten by an eagle, so be it.

Just to be bossy I made myself stern. "Ok, you can stay, but you have to copy your spelling words, then you can collect some more figs, a whole bucket and don't leave the clearing or go up on the rocks. You promise?"

"Sure," Jacob answered going back to his game. "Chuga. Chuga. Chuga. Woooo, woooo!" He made all the right noises even though his locomotive was only a long row of stones.

"I mean it." I hid a smile. He might be dirty and wild but he was still cute.

As usual, the first thing I did was check on the flags. All were still standing. I gazed out to sea. No boats. No aircraft. With a sinking heart, I wondered if there even was a search party. Maybe they'd already given up. If that was the case, it was my fault; I should have thought of the flags earlier.

Down on the beach, expecting to be disappointed again, I approached the trap slowly, but for once I was surprised. A lone fish, silver and black and about a foot long, was circling in the pool, looking for a way to get out. I ran for the handmade wooden spear Jacob had made and we'd stored between the big rocks. Never having killed anything bigger than a spider, I was scared.

"Thank you for your life," I said to the fish, the way my Grandpa told me the Native Americans did when they hunted. It took me seven stabs before I got him.

"Oh, my gosh! Oh, my gosh!" I shouted as the silver fish wiggled and flashed at the end of my stick. "What should I do now?" Finally I took one of the stones at the side of the trap and knocked him out.

"Food!" I yelled, laughing. "Me great hunter!" I couldn't wait to show Jacob, but first I had to clean the fish. The guts aren't edible.

Our dad went fly-fishing up in the mountains of West Virginia and I knew that fish have to be cleaned properly, so I pulled out the hunting knife I now kept in a leather holder on one of the homesteader's belts. This was going to be gross!

HOW TO CLEAN A FISH

Step one: If the fish has scales, like most fish do
scrape them off with a sharp knife.

Step two: Take the knife and cut off the head.

Step three: Slice the fish along its bottom edge.

Step four: Scoop the guts out with your finger.

(This is the part I was most afraid of, but the fish had hardly any blood.)

CHAPTER 15

STORM

By the time I got back to the cabin, the sky was boiling with dark purple clouds.

"Jacob," I called, looking all around for him. His train-rocks were still arranged on the floor, but there was no answer.

"Jacob!" I yelled standing on the porch, scanning the clearing. A few of the nanny goats looked up and came over.

"Does anyone know where Jacob is?" I asked as if the goats could understand. "Did anyone see where he went?" The animals continued to graze.

Only a few moments ago I was so excited to show Jacob our first fish, now I was mad. If I were a cartoon character smoke would be coming out my ears. I wrapped the precious fish in a clean cloth and got out a bucket. It was time to milk the nannies and I would have to do it all by myself. Mother Goat and Midnight were waiting by the porch.

"Darn it! Why didn't he stay where I told him?" I asked the nannies as I sat on the homesteader's old wooden milking stool. "I have half a mind to let him find his own way home, but if the storm hits and he's lost or in trouble I would never forgive myself. This must be what it feels like to be a parent when your kids won't mind."

"Jacob!" I called from the top of a big boulder when I took the jars of warm milk to the spring.

"Jacob!" Where could he be? And why wouldn't he answer? I was starting to get a bad feeling.

"Beyaaaaaaa."

What was that? Somewhere, nearby, a mother goat was bleating.

"Beyaaaaaa... eyaaaaa..." Every few minutes, I heard the cry. "Eayaaaaaaaaaa." I imagined Jacob at the nanny's side.

"EEEEEAAAAAAAA." The goat's cries were louder now.

"JACOB!" I shouted.

"Here." His small voice came from a big crack in the rocks; then I saw him lying on his stomach next to a nanny. The brown and white animal had a big swollen belly. I'd seen her waddling around the grassy clearing just yesterday, pawing the ground and acting edgy.

I crawled into the hollow. "Didn't you hear me call?"

"Not until now. I was collecting a bucket of figs when this mother goat started crying and I followed her here. She's in trouble." It was then that I noticed that only one of the unborn kid's feet was sticking out.

"What are you doing?" I demanded staring at my brother as he pulled his hand out of the nanny goat's backside.

"This baby is coming out wrong, just like the first one, the one that died. See?"

My little brother amazed me. One rainy day when we couldn't go outside, I'd read aloud the chapter of the book that told what to do when a nanny had a difficult labor. It described how sometimes shepherds had to go inside and pull out a foot. Jacob didn't seem to be listening, but he must have been, because now he was trying to do what the book said.

"Can you feel the other hoof?"

"Yes, but just the tip. Your fingers are longer. You try."

"Bleeeee!" cried the mother goat, humping up again and again. "Bleeee!" she cried in the most pitiful way. "I need help!" was what she was saying.

It had started to rain and the wind whipped the bushes and small trees back and forth, but here in the narrow overhang, we were still dry.

"Ok..." I said as I slowly pushed up my sleeves. "I'll

try, but this is going to be gross."

"Beyaaaaa," said the nanny as she strained again and again. If the baby goat couldn't come out, it would die inside her and then the nanny would get infected and die too.

First, I held my hands outside the cave and washed them in the rainwater. Soap would be better, but our birth kit was back at the cabin. "Move over," I told Jacob. Then, lying down on my side, I slowly wormed my fingers into the mother's birth canal. "I can feel the other foot!"

"Can you pull it out?"

"Give me one of your shoe laces."

"What for? Are you going to get it all gooey?"

"It will wash."

Jacob did as I said and I started making a knot like a noose. "This is how they showed it in the book. If I can get the noose around the foot, you can pull." In another few minutes, I'd found the lost hoof and attached the loop of shoestring.

"Ok, pull when the mother goat strains, but gently." I had no idea if this would work. Jacob waited for the next push, while I lay on the ground with my hand still inside the mother. When she strained, he pulled and I tried to make room for the second foot. Finally both feet showed at the opening and I wanted to cheer, but

I didn't because a loud noise would scare the mother.

"Careful. Careful... Pull slowly when she pushes... Come on mother, you can help us. Come on now!" I encouraged her.

The brown and white goat glanced over. She could tell her baby wasn't stuck anymore and a look of hope came into her eyes. "Bleeeaaa," she said. Then again, Beyaaaaaaaaa!" Now she was pushing with all her heart and there was the baby kid's nose!

"BEYAAAAAAAAA!" The mother bellowed and an all white baby was out on the grass. Jacob took off his shirt and wiped the little goat's face and pushed it close to its mother. "Lets call her Snowball," he said.

"Bleaaaa," said the Mama goat as she grunted one more time and we were astonished when a second baby slid out, right in front of us! The little mother had given birth to twins! This one was white with black spots and Jacob named it Polka Dot.

"You know what, Trill?" he asked, not waiting for an answer. "We are goat midwives!" This made me smile and I knew it would make our Mom and Grandma Jean proud.

As we watched the babies find their mother's milk, a wind came up and began to howl. It was like a living thing that wanted to sweep the whole island clean. Thunder crashed and then heavy rain came. It crashed so close it shook the gray rocks. Next lightning lit the whole sky. Back and forth, thunder and lightning, like in a war zone.

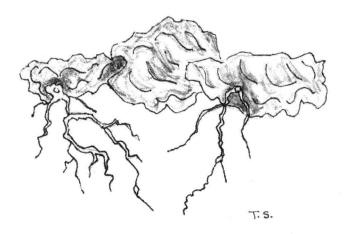

T.S.

"Let's not try to go home," Jacob said and I agreed, so we curled up with the contented nanny and her twins under the overhang and tried to sleep.

All night the storm raged and I imagined our signal flags had probably blown down. All night it rained and there was more thunder and lightning. Lightning and thunder. In the dark hours another goat moved in and by the smell I could tell it was a male, but it wasn't King Billy. It was the Duke!

"Hello," Jacob said, rolling over and rubbing the big animal's wet fur. "Maybe he's the twins father."

The Duke licked Jacob's face. I was shocked. More

than any of the other goats, The Duke seemed wild and fierce, like he didn't want to be friends... Now I knew I was wrong. Slowly I reached out my hand.

CHAPTER 16

BEACHCOMBING

AFTER THE BIG STORM, IT TOOK HALF A DAY TO FIND THE SIGNAL FLAGS AND GET THEM BACK IN POSITION. There were now 44 notches on the walking stick.

"Do you think we'll live here forever?" Jacob surprised me by asking.

"Yeah, we will be like two old hermits," I joked. "You'll have a long beard and I'll have scraggly white wild hair." I put on my straw hat, hunched my shoulders and stomped around the cabin looking like a witch, with a scowl on my face, to make him laugh, but really I was beginning to wonder. Would we live here forever?

Every day we checked the flags and went down to the fish trap. Sometimes there was one fish. Sometimes there were two or three. Sometimes the pool was empty. When there were no fish we combed the beach for useful items and found a soccer ball and an old net. I started collecting shells again. One morning we found two long boards.

"Oh, no!" Jacob whined, "This is too hard!"

It was a hot day. We were halfway up the cliff dragging the boards behind us, sweating and breathing hard.

"This will take forever!" he continued.

For just a moment, I thought of slapping him, but I was immediately ashamed. How could I be so mean? He was just a little boy.

"It's ok, Jacob," I changed my attitude, which wasn't easy for a person like me. "We'll stop a few times before we get to the top and after that it will be level. You never know, someday we may be very happy we went to this trouble, all for two long boards."

When we got up to the bluff, we lay on the rocks and looked out over the water. "You know what I call this place in my head, Jacob?" I asked.

"Goat Island?" That made me laugh.

"No. Hope Island. I've called it Hope Island since almost the beginning, because I don't want to lose hope."

"Good idea," Jacob said. "I don't want you to lose hope either."

"What about you? Do you ever feel hopeless?" I asked him.

"No. I just keep going, day by day and I think that whatever happens we'll be ok," Jacob said.

Sometimes my little brother amazed me. He's younger than me, but he seems so wise.

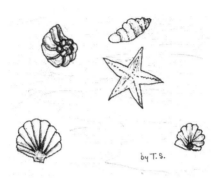

by T.S.

When we got home, I was in a good mood. "I'm going to learn how to make cheese," I said. "In the back of the goat book, I found a pamphlet that gives directions and we have everything we need; milk, vinegar and a screened sieve that the homesteaders left."

What we ended up with wasn't anything like cheese you get in the store. It was kind of rubbery but it was good and I was proud of it.

Little by little our diet was expanding. We had figs, berries and wild greens (sorrel, watercress and dandelion leaves). We had milk and cheese and fish. It was plain food and boring, but we were full and eventually I thought we'd start getting our weight back.

HOW TO MAKE CHEESE

First, boil 2 cups of milk and put in five teaspoons of vinegar.

If you have salt you can add some, but we didn't have any.

Let the milk sit over night.

It will make little curds like cottage cheese.

Pour the liquid and curds through a sieve

If you don't have a sieve, use a clean cloth.

Squish out all the liquid. This is called whey.

Let the curds sit some more. Now you have cottage cheese.

If you want, you can mold the cheese into a ball.

Put the cheese in a jar and keep it cool in a spring.

Give the whey back to the goats.

They will love it.

By T. S.

BEE LINE

"Look, another bee!" Jacob said one day when we were collecting greens. It was a warm afternoon and the scent of wild flowers filled the air. The bee was sitting on a yellow blossom that looked like a daisy.

"Watch out! Don't bother it," I warned.

Jacob studied the insect as it picked bits of orange fuzz from the center of the flower and with its tiny legs rubbed the orange all over his body. "Look. It's collecting pollen to take back to its hive. The colony must be nearby," he said. I leaned down to look as the bee took off in a straight line toward the high boulders.

"Up there," Jacob yelled as he set down his bucket and we ran after it. Five times we lost sight of the bee. Then, half way up a pitted cliff, we heard buzzing. High over our heads, dozens of the insects were flying in and out of a hole in the rocks.

"That's their hive!" Jacob was really excited. "The bees make tiny wax boxes, the size of the tip of your finger and connect them together. It's called comb and they fill it with honey."

"I know." I said. "We ate some honeycomb at Grandma's, remember?"

Jacob stared at the opening where the bees flew in and out, "I wish we could get some! It makes my mouth water."

"It would be really hard," I said, smelling the sweet air that came from the cave. "The opening's so small, the bees will attack us if we try to get in."

"I could do it," Jacob whispered. He wanted that honey.

I shook my head. I was more afraid. "It's getting dark. We know where the bees live now. We can come back tomorrow. Let's go back to the clearing and get our buckets of greens." I pulled on my brother's shirt. He was still working out how to get the honey.

"Tomorrow," I said again. "I promise."

All night I thought about the honey and I dreamed about it too. The brown sugar the homesteaders left hadn't lasted long and like most kids we loved sweets. For over a month we hadn't had any.

It was weird. At home we could have any kind of food we wanted: big salads and homemade cookies and ice cream, peanut butter and granola. We could go to restaurants or drive-thru places.

Here we had six things, figs, berries, wild greens, fish, milk and now cheese. We didn't even have salt and pepper.

Before it was light, I got up and lit a candle. The more I thought about it, I wanted honey as bad as Jacob did. Standing on tiptoe, I reached for a heavy book on the homesteader's highest shelf, one I'd never opened before called *The Life of the Honey Bee*.

It was the beekeeper's outfit I was interested in. If I could protect Jacob from stings I could let him go into the cave with a bucket. Thumbing through the pages, I searched for pictures.

Jacob sat up in bed. "What are you doing? It's still dark outside."

"Trying to figure out how to make a bee suit. See." I carried the book and the candle to the bed. "The man is completely protected. There's an old long sleeved shirt in the metal trunk you could wear and we could tuck your long pants into your socks, but we need gloves for your hands. I guess the homesteader's old stiff leather gloves will have to do." I showed him a photo of the man in a white suit and veiled hat, opening a white wooden beehive.

"We have your old straw hat." Jacob pointed to where it hung on a wooden peg.

"But what could we use for a veil?" I wondered.

Jacob studied the picture, threw back the covers and got down on the floor. He pulled something out from under the bed. It was the remains of the old canvas tent that we'd cut apart to make flags. "See, it has netting where the door was!"

By mid-morning, I had the suit and hat ready. "And guess what else I learned in the bee book?" I asked my little brother who was standing on a stool washing up our breakfast bowls at the sink. "If we make a fire near the hive, the bees will smell it and suck up as much honey as they can. They'll think there's going to be a wildfire and get ready to save their winter supplies. After they've stuffed themselves full of honey, it's harder for them to sting. That's why beekeepers use a smoker to keep the bees from stinging them."

Jacob was so excited he danced around the room. "When can we go? Can we leave now?"

CHAPTER 17

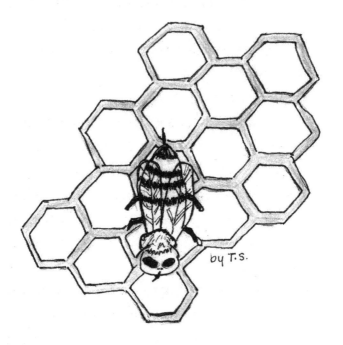

by T·S·

HONEY ROBBERS

By the time the sun was at the top of the sky, we were prepared. I rolled the bee outfit up in the pack, put my straw hat on my brother's head and got a clean bucket for the honey. Jacob was so happy to be going on this adventure that he began to sing. "The bees go flying one by one, hurray! Hurray!" But I was scared because I knew this was risky. People can die if they're stung too many times or if they have an allergic reaction.

As usual, a troop of young goats followed us, skipping and hopping over the small boulders. When they got near the cave Jacob shooed them away. Above, we could see the bees still flying in and out of the hole and hear the soft buzz.

"It's higher than I remembered," I said.

"If I can stand on your shoulders, I can crawl in," Jacob thought out-loud as he got dressed in his suit.

I shook my head. "This is one of the most dangerous things we've done since we got here and it's going to be hard. I can only hold you for a few minutes. As soon as you get in, I'll hand you the bucket and then I'll hand you the torch."

While Jacob tucked the heavy shirt with long sleeves into the droopy pants and tightened the veil, I wrapped an old rag around a stick and gave him two wooden matches.

"You'll have to light this torch to make smoke once you get in. Can you do that? The matches are precious and we can't afford to waste them."

"I think I can."

Finally, I got ready to do my part by pressing myself against the rock wall. There were ridges in the boulder that I could hold on to.

"Sorry," Jacob said as he used my body for a ladder. To get up, he pulled on my clothes and tugged at my arms. It was good he was small and not too heavy. Once on my shoulders, he was able to slide into the hole, which was about the size of a basketball hoop.

Standing on my toes, I held up the bucket with the hunting knife in it, along with the torch and the matches. After that my little brother disappeared into the dark. Meanwhile the buzzing grew louder.

What have I done? I sent my little brother into a black hole full of dangerous insects. If the bees attack Jacob, I have no way to get him out and all for a bucket of honey!

"Damn!" I hear my little brother yell.

"Jacob! Don't swear."

"My first match went out, anyway dad swears. Grandpa swears. Even Grandma, sometimes." Lordy, I think. He's going to be a handful if we have to stay on Hope Island much longer!

A few seconds later, I hear another match strike and this time light flickers at the opening.

"Everything ok?" No answer. "Jacob?"

"Wow! You should see this. The whole roof is covered with yellow honeycomb. It looks like a gold mine." For the next few minute, there's nothing but the scraping of the bucket as it's moved across the cave floor. Then, "Ow! Ow!" Jacob yells. 'The bees have found a way to get into my bee-suit. Ow!"

The next thing I know, the flaming torch flies out of the cave. It sputters and goes out when it hits the ground. Then Jacob's hat and veil show at the opening.

"Ow! They're stinging me. Here. Take this. Hurry!" he squeals, leaning forward and dangling the honey-bucket. "I'm coming!"

Again, by standing on my toes, I can just reach, but the pail is so heavy I almost drop it. That would be awful! Quickly I set it down in a safe place. I push myself under him and let him slide down my body. My poor little brother!

But Jacob is laughing. "Wow! You should have seen inside that cave! I might be the only person that's ever been in there. Wow!" He throws off his hat and slaps at his head. A bee is tangled in his curly brown hair.

"Wow! Ow!" Jacob strips off the rest of his heavy clothes, brushes off a few more insects and stands in his undershorts. He's still laughing. I gather our things in the backpack and we hurry away as fast as we can before the bees come after us.

"Honey Robbers. That's what we are!" Jacob yells and does a crazy dance.

By now, I am laughing too. "Honey robbers!"

That night, supper was berries and honey, figs and honey, cheese and honey.

CHAPTER 18

A KNOCK AT THE DOOR

LIGHT WAS JUST CREEPING UNDER THE WHITE CURTAINS WHEN I HEARD A LOUD RAP ON THE DOOR. THUMP. THUMP.

Jacob and I sat up in bed and looked at each other. As far we knew we were the only humans on the island and though for almost two months we'd survived on our own, we'd always believed that sooner or later someone would come for us.

The knock came again, sharp and loud. Thump. Thump.

"Who could it be?" Jacob whispered. "Maybe it's Dad with a search party! I knew there was hope!"

I put one finger to my lips, then, silent as a shadow, crept to the window, but no one was there.

Thump. Thump. The knock came again, only louder.

"I guess we better answer," I said as I unbolted the door and cracked it open.

The huge white billy goat, with the big dangerous

looking curved horns and fierce yellow eyes, stood on the porch.

"King Billy!" I exclaimed and turned to my brother. "Why would he come to our door like this?"

"Beeeeya," he bleated. "BEEEEYA." He looked over his shoulder across the clearing and I heard in my mind, one word. Danger.

"What is it?" I asked the big Billy.

The goat's yellow eyes blazed and he turned and trotted toward the jungle gym tree. I scanned the sky. A few stars were still out, but there were no clouds. It was going to be a hot day and a storm wasn't coming. What could The King want?

"I guess we have to follow him," I said, but Jacob was ahead of me. He'd already pulled on his pants and shoes and was on his way out the door. "Wait" I called. "I'm coming too."

The fierce goat trotted toward the center of the clearing. He passed the dead pine tree that the little goats played on and stopped where half-a-dozen nannies and kids were standing in a circle looking down. I hoped it wasn't another dead baby goat. The day the first baby goat died was a really sad day.

"Beeeeeeeeeeeeeya! Beeeeeeeeeya!" The goats in the circle were bleating and there was an answer from a distance... "Beeeeeeya."

"Where's that cry coming from?" Jacob asks.

"It sounds so far away. Maybe a goat is trapped in one of the ravines between the huge rocks."

As King Billy leads us into the circle, the animals step away and we look down. There's a hole in the ground about three feet wide that we've never seen before. Old boards and dead grass must have covered it, but something has fallen through.

"Beeeeeeeeya!" We hear the cry again, almost under our feet.

"It's an old well," I observe, leaning down to look. "The people who lived here must have dug it. Maybe the wooden cover was rotten and one of the little goats fell through."

Jacob kneels down to look, but I grip his shirt. "Be careful! The last thing we need is two kids in a well!" I think this is funny because little goats are called kids and Jacob is a kid, but he doesn't laugh and none of the goats have a sense of humor, certainly not King Billy who is always regal and stern.

"How are we going to get him out?" Jacob wonders. "Do you think there's water down there? Can goats swim?"

"I don't know. I once saw an elk swim across a river

in a nature show. Let's drop a rock down and see if we hear a splash." Jacob looks around, comes back with a handful of rocks and drops them all in.

"Beeeeeya!" complains the kid in the bottom, but we hear a splash, so we know there has to be at least a few inches of water.

"I'm going to get the clothesline from the cabin and drop it down so we can see how deep the well and water are," I explain. "You stay here and talk to the little goat so he won't be afraid."

I run to the back of the stone house and untie the clothesline, then I hurry back to find Jacob leaning into the well again. He's calling down to the frightened kid, "It's ok. We're going to rescue you. Don't worry."

JACOB'S LADDER

To figure out the depth of the well, we tie a stick to the bottom of the rope, and then slowly lower it into the hole until it hits something.

"Beeeeya!"

"That must be the goat," Jacob observes. "Wiggle it around so we can see if there's water further down. Maybe the well's partly caved in."

I try what he says. Sometimes, he's a very smart boy.

126

The rope with the stick sinks a little further and then stops. When I pull it up, five feet at the bottom are wet. The young goat must be standing on a ledge about half way down.

"Now how do we get him out? It's not going to be easy. We could build a ladder, but we don't have any poles and there aren't any tall trees."

"How about those long boards we found on the beach after the storm? Let's go look in the shed. Maybe there's some other stuff... We'll be right back little goat," Jacob adds.

Across the meadow, we jog to the recess in the rocks where we store valuable things and within a few minutes we locate the two long boards and a piece of fishnet.

"We can use the net to haul the little goat up," Jacob says.

"But what can we use for cross pieces on the ladder?" I wonder out loud.

"What about that wooden pad we saw on the beach. The one you said cargo ships use to store stuff. It was too heavy to bring back, but we could take our hammer and pry some of the narrow boards off," Jacob says. "Let's go. We can check our rescue flags and our fish trap while we're down there."

A few hours later we are back in the clearing. My brother places the short boards across the long boards about every two feet and I nail them down. It's so hot sweat drips in my eyes. When the ladder's finally finished, we carry it over to the well. The young goat has stopped crying and all the other goats have gone off to graze.

"Do you think the little kid could be dead?" Jacob asks, leaning down to look into the black hole.

"Be careful, Jacob! If one of us has an accident there's no hospital or doctor and if you fall in I don't want to have to clean up your bloody body!"

This is said as a joke, but it's true. I still hate blood and I still fear the dark. Now I'm about to go down into the deep black hole. It's too hard for Jacob and if the water is five-feet-deep it would be over his head.

"There's one other thing; the wild goats are our friends, but they aren't tame. The little kid will probably struggle when I wrap it in the net and it will struggle when we try to pull it out. So be prepared."

Slowly and carefully, my brother and I insert the ladder. It's hard work because the wood is so heavy and it's so hot we are sweating like pigs. I fold the fishnet, stick it down my jeans then sit on the side and drop my feet on the first rung. My insides are shaking, but I remember how brave Jacob was when he climbed into the bee cave to collect the honey. He laughed at danger.

THE DEEP BLACK HOLE

Half way down the ladder, I look up. Like a full moon in the daytime sky, Jacob's face shines above me. Below, I can hear a weak "beyaaa," so at least the little goat is still alive. With each rung the light at the top of the well gets dimmer and Jacob gets further away. I begin to breathe hard and try not to think about spiders and snakes. I can face almost any creature in the light, but in the dark it's something else.

"I'm coming," I say. "I'm coming."

It's on the bottom rung that the ladder slips sideways. I try to hold on, but the next thing I know I'm under water. It's dark and cold and I feel like I'm drowning in the ocean again, but I push up with my feet and find that by standing on tiptoe I can keep my mouth and nose in the air. I want to yell for help, but there's no one to help me.

Looking up, the circle of light seems very far away and I can't see Jacob's face anymore.

"Are you ok?" he calls down.

"Yeah. I'm in the water though. The little goat is right in front of me. Guess who it is! Little X. Throw down the rope. I'm going to climb up on the ledge where he's sitting and try to wrap him up in the net."

The trick will be to keep the animal from trying to get away. No person or animal likes to be tied up. Little X is one of our favorites, but he can be wild and he's strong.

To keep us both calm, I sing a lullaby while I worked. "To my little one's bedside in the night. Comes a new little goat snowy white." Jacob sings with me. "The goat will trot to the market-while mother her watch does keep..." It was the song our mother used to sing... when we had a mother. A tear comes to my eye, but I brush it away. No time for that now.

"How're you doing?" Jacob calls. "Here comes the rope."

"Ok," I call up to him a few minutes later. "I've got Little X in the net bag and the rope tied on. I'm going to put him over my shoulder... We need to straighten the ladder. Can you reach it?" Tilting my head back I can see my little brother's brown hands stretching into the well, but his arms are too short. "That's alright. Wait. No! Don't lean down any further. I'll try something else." For once he obeys me.

Using my shoulder, I began to push the ladder to the side. Little by little I get it straight. "I'm coming up now. Hold the rope, but don't pull until I get part way up, then we can lift Little X out together."

I'm half way up when I hear the wood splinter... With all my might, I cling to the rung above me. Crack! The rung under my feet splits and breaks. Splash! I slip back into the water again.

This time the tears came for real and I'm sure my leg is bleeding.

"You ok?" Jacob yells down. "Trillium, you ok?"

I take a deep breath. "Yeah." I yell back, but to tell the truth, I'm not ok. What if every rung breaks and I'm trapped in the dark hole forever? I shake my head to get rid of such thoughts and try again.

This time I have to pull my self and Little X from the first rung to the third rung, a big stretch. I just hope it will hold me and it does. "Ok, now, Jacob, start pulling Little X up. Gently. Gently!"

As the rope tightens, some of the weight of the young goat on my shoulders lifts and he swings away from me. The light gets closer! Finally, I wipe the sweat from my eyes and peek over the edge. Daylight has never been so welcome.

"Yay!" yells Jacob and helps me out of the well.

"Beeeeeya!" call all the goats that have come down to see what's happening.

As soon as I'm out, we begin to pull the rope the rest of the way up and I can feel Little X struggle.

"Beeeeya," his cry gets louder. Mother Goat trots over and looks down the well.

"Beeeeeeeeeeya!" she calls her kid. Soon we can actually see the little goat's head and when we untie him, he runs to his Mom. He wants to nurse for comfort and though he's too big, Mother Goat lets him.

"We did it!" Jacob crows. "Sometimes when there aren't any grown-ups around, kids can do more than anyone would expect." Above us three golden eagles circle. "We can do anything, if we have to." he says. "We can do anything but fly!"

CHAPTER 19

by T. S.

MYSTERY

By the time we're done taking the ladder apart and using the boards to make a new well cover, the shadows stretch long across the clearing and a strong wind has come up. The hot day suddenly feels cool, almost cold, and I shiver.

"I'm starved," Jacob says. "We've been working since early this morning and we never even had breakfast. I'm going to make dried berries mixed with cottage cheese and honey for dinner."

"I'll go to the spring to get a jar of cold cottage cheese while you milk the nannies," I say.

By the time I get back, Jacob is sitting on the porch, looking very sad. "What's wrong?"

"It's gone, all gone, our beautiful golden honey."

"What do you mean gone? How can it be gone? Did the goats get it? Was the lid still on? Was the stone on top of the lid where we left it last night?"

"Yes, the stone was on top," Jacob answers. "But there's no honey in the bucket, just some hard old brown stuff. No honey at all." He's almost crying.

I don't believe it! The bucket looks undisturbed, but when I peek in, Jacob's right. The honey is gone. Not a lick remains. A hard brown material is in its place.

"Where's all the golden honeycomb? How can this be?" I sit down on the step above my brother to puzzle it out. As far as we know, Jacob and I are the only humans here. It's unlikely a new person has come to the cabin, found the honey, and replaced it with the brown stuff. Why would he or she do that? If he wanted the honey, why not take the whole bucket and run?

If the thief was a goat, say one of the big ones, like King Billy or the Duke, he would just knock the lid off with his horns and lick up the honey. I look in the bucket again and frown. After all the hard work and courage it took for Jacob to get the honey, it's gone! The brown shiny stuff in the bucket is as hard as wood.

I poke it with a stick. Hard and tough. I poke it again. How could this be!

Poke! Poke! Poke! I'm losing my temper, but I can't help it. Whack! I kick the bucket across the stone steps.

"Trillium, stop!" That's Jacob. He's catches the bucket as it rolls toward him. I think he's telling me to stop because I'm getting so angry, but that isn't it. "Look, Trill, look! The honey is still here!"

"Right!" I say, thinking he's teasing.

"No, really!" He carries the bucket back up the steps. "Look," he repeats, tipping it sideways. "The brown junk cracked when the bucket rolled down the steps and the good golden honey is oozing through!"

"What could have happened?" I pull out my hunting knife and lift up the hard brown mass. "It's a chunk of wax about four inches thick. In the heat of the day, the honeycomb must have melted and floated to the top. Then when the air cooled, the wax hardened again, covering the honey."

We look at each other. We are rich again, rich in honey, something better than gold.

At sunset, we fall asleep without reading a story. Our stomachs are full and our bodies are tired from all our hard work. The honey, in clear clean glass jars, sits on the highest shelf of the cupboard and Little X sleeps safely next to his mother.

BUTTER

In the following days, nothing much changed. Each morning we milked the nannies that stood patiently waiting outside the cabin. Mother Goat, Midnight and the other white female that we helped have the twins seemed to like to be milked and we needed the food, so we were happy to do it. There were other nanny goats that had milk, but they were too wild to be touched.

From the homesteader's books I learned how to make butter. It's easy and we took turns churning the milk, sitting out on the porch, singing, "Day-o, day-ay-ay-o, daylight comes and I want to go home." It's an old work song banana pickers used to sing that we learned from Grandpa Pete. "Come, Mister tally man, tally my bananas. Daylight come and I want to go home." When we got to the last part we sang real loud. "Daylight comes and I want to go home!"

In the afternoon, we gathered wood and each day we had to go further and further from the clearing to find it. After that, Jacob did his lessons and I washed clothes or mended them with the home-

T.S.

136

steader's needle and thread. I'd never sewed anything before, but I taught myself how. Our clothes and our shoes were in very bad shape and needed constant repairing.

When I thought about it, I was sure that if we hadn't found the cabin for shelter and the books that taught us how to survive, we would have starved in a few weeks. Starved and died. I shook my head. I just had to stay positive and believe that one of these days help would come.

How to Make Your Own Butter

First you let fresh milk sit over night in a jar.
In the morning you scoop off the thick cream on top.
Put the cream in a jar and shake it for a long time.
(It takes about an hour so don't get discouraged.)
Pretty soon tiny flecks of yellow
will begin to show in the whipped cream.
When the flecks of gold get bigger,
pour the liquid through a piece of clean cloth or a sieve
and press the butter into a cup.
You can add salt, but we didn't have any.
Do not throw the liquid away.
It is buttermilk and good to drink.

CHAPTER 20

DISCOVERY

ONE DAY WHEN WE'D FINISHED OUR CHORES, JACOB MADE A SUGGESTION. "Lets go explore the other side of the island. We haven't been there in a long time." I wasn't in the mood and had planned to spend the afternoon working on my drawings.

This was a project I'd started weeks ago when I was thinking about our parents. In an old watercolor tablet I'd found in the bottom of the metal chest, I was drawing pictures of the things I saw and of some of our adventures.

Sometimes I spent hours on one detailed image, other times it was just a sketch. I drew the goats, the cliffs, the cabin and the clearing. In case we died, whoever came after us would know how hard we had tried to survive.

I was thinking bad thoughts again and I shook them out of my head. "Ok, Jacob. Maybe we should go out. Maybe we'll see something new. Get your napsack and

I'll bring the canteen."

The sacks were made of pant legs from the home-steader's old clothes. We took them everywhere, in case we found food and we always brought the home-steader's metal canteen with us, because so far we'd only found two springs on the island and one of them was going dry.

For a good hour, we wound around and over boul-ders as big as the cabin. In some places the trail was well worn, other times you couldn't see it. On top of the rocks, we could keep our eyes on the sun as it trav-eled across the sky, but when we dropped into the ra-vines it was like a maze and easy to get lost. Finally, we came to a drop-off where the ocean spread out before us.

I knew that somewhere across the sea people were going about their lives. Kids were riding bikes, watch-ing TV or playing video games. Soldiers were fighting. Parents were driving to work or riding the train, but here was a different world with no sounds but the gulls and the waves breaking on the shore. We walked along the cliff looking for a path down to the beach.

"Don't forget, once we get down there, we have to get up again," I warned, but before I could say more, Ja-cob found a smooth boulder that was almost like a slide and sat down. He landed on his bottom in the sand.

A GREAT FIND

"That was cool!" Jacob called up. "You try it." So I slid down too.

"Look," I said, staring down. "The sand is green with dark gray stones all around, very different from the white sandy beach with the fish trap."

Mixed in with the rocks were bright red and blue plastic bags that at first I thought were deflated balloons. Jacob picked one up.

"Trillium!" he yelled. "It's a bag of potato chips!" He was ripping it open.

"Wait! Let me see if they're any good."

"They are good! Still salty and crisp." He was already stuffing the chips into his mouth. I picked up another bag. The plastic was still sealed and full of air, that's why they'd floated onto the beach. The red and blue bags were a treasure! There were more still bobbing up and down in the surf, all kinds of them, potato chips and corn chips, spicy chips and plain!

For a long while we sat on the sand eating them by the handfuls, then we slowed down. The salt made us thirsty and we drank all the cold spring water from our canteen.

"Let's get the rest of the bags," Jacob said. So we waded out after every last one.

"I guess we better go back to the clearing and milk the goats. Let's pick up as many bags of as we can and store the rest at the top. After we milk we can come back and get them."

"Where do you think the chips came from?" Jacob wondered.

"Maybe they washed off a cargo ship."

We made three more trips and by dark we had one hundred and four bags stored in the shed. 104!

by T.S.

CHAPTER **21**

THE CHIP DISASTER

"Wake up, Trillium," Jacob whispered. "Something's wrong."

"What?" I didn't feel so good. My mouth was dry and my stomach churned.

"It's the goats. Listen."

"Beeeeeya. Beeeya. Bleeeeeeeeeeeeee."

He crossed the bare floor and kneeled on a chair to see out the window. "Come look. They're circling the clearing, crying to each other. We'd better go check. While we're out, we can get some more chips for breakfast."

"You've got to be kidding! My mouth is so salty, I can hardly swallow." I pushed myself up in bed. "The goats do sound funny."

"Aieeeeee!" they were crying. "Bleeeeya! Bleeeeeeeee!" in high and low voices. We went out barefoot to look.

"Ow!" I stepped on a sticker and when I bent down, I

noticed a piece of red plastic tangled in the grass. Looking around the meadow, I saw blue and red litter everywhere. Some of the goats were lying down moaning, others were crying like they were trying to have a baby. Even King Billy's head hung low and he had a piece of the red plastic stuck in his beard. Jacob ran for the shed.

"Oh no!" he yelled. The barrel where we'd stored the chips was empty. Not only that, there was a trail of torn red and blue plastic leading out to the meadow. By the time I caught up with him, he had started to cry. "We were going to have chips for breakfast!" he yelled and kicked the old wooden barrel. Then he kicked it again.

"Don't be so selfish. Look at the goats. They've eaten all the chips and the bags too. Now they're sick and in pain."

It was true. The goats were all standing with their

mouths open, their heads drooping down and their backs hunched up. Each one was suffering. Some of the little ones were trying to go to the bathroom, but nothing was coming out. Little X was one of them. King Billy was up on a rock but facing away. He wasn't guarding the herd anymore. He had his own problems.

Not worrying about my bare feet or getting stickers in them, I ran for the house. I flung open the door and went for the book about goats, the one we used to learn how to milk and how to help mother goats when they had difficulty giving birth to their babies. The herd had always seemed so healthy. Now maybe they were dying.

The first thing I did was look for a chapter on sickness and what to do. The news was not good. The book described what we'd just seen. Goats that were bloated and crying were very ill. If they didn't care about playing or eating, they were very ill.

The book said that goats in cartoons could gobble down anything, tin cans and long underwear off clotheslines. But real goats were sensitive and got upset stomachs and dehydrated easily. Unfortunately the goat book didn't tell you what to do about it, except telephone an animal doctor right away, but that wasn't going to happen.

I closed the book and looked out the window.

Mother goat was standing near the porch waiting to be milked, but she had vomited all over the ground. Her tongue was hanging out of her mouth like she was thirsty. I felt thirsty too and wished I hadn't eaten all those chips. While I thought about their sickness, I went to the bucket by the sink and got a cup of water. That gave me an idea...

"Jacob!" I yelled from the front porch. For once he came running. "The book said goats are not hardy. They can adapt over time, but will get ill if their diet changes suddenly. The author also says that goats can die fast if not treated. The loss of the tasty chips was a bad break for us, but losing all the goats would be worse. We depend on them for milk and cheese." I don't say the rest... And if the goats die, we might die too.

"So here's my idea. Remember Grandma Jean used to say that water is the best medicine. She told us that people could live with out food for weeks, but not witout water and that half the illnesses people have could be cured by drinking pure water?"

"I guess..."

"Well, we don't have any medicine for the goats and we don't really know what's wrong with them, but they might be sick because they ate all the chips and some of the plastic is stuck in their stomachs or throats. I think we should get them to drink a lot of water. I'm thirsty, aren't you?"

"Yeah...."

"Well, let's bring the water to them in a bucket. They're too weak to get to the spring."

All morning, until the sun was high in the sky, we went back and forth to the pool. We started with the baby goats first, filling jars from the bucket and giving each one a big drink. With the sicker ones, I held their heads up and Jacob poured two cups of water down their throats.

Sometimes I felt like giving up. My plan didn't seem to be working. The most pitiful goats were now lying on their sides, moaning. Their cries of "Aieeeee!" had stopped, but this was not a good sign. They were too weak to cry.

The last goat to get water was King Billy high up on the boulder. It was hard to bring the bucket all the way up to him and when we did, he wouldn't even lift his head. (Though I actually thought of the big male goat as a friend, I was still afraid of him.)

"Danger....." I heard him say as we approached, but it was only a whisper. I knew what he meant. He was dying. Since he was the biggest, he had probably eaten the most chips. Goats were wonderful companions, but sometimes they weren't very smart.

Timidly, we lifted his head. Carefully we poured two cups down his throat. Then because he was the biggest, we gave him two more. Afterward we sat with him and Jacob petted his head and his long curved horns. We had never before been this close to the King.

"Hey, what about the Duke?" I asked. "He isn't with the herd."

"We better look for him!" Jacob was already heading toward the center of the island. I looked down into the clearing. Most of the goats were still lying on their sides, but a few raised their heads and were looking around. It was hard to tell if the water cure was working, but if Jacob was leaving I better keep up, so I filled the canteen from the bucket and followed.

PRAYER

The Duke was wild and sometimes unfriendly, but he had saved Jacob's life when the golden eagle attacked. The two of us looked in all the places we knew. We went to the clearing where we'd first met the goats. We went to the cave in the rocks where we'd helped the nanny have her baby in the middle of a thunderstorm. We climbed to the highest point of the island, a jumble of granite boulders bigger than houses with cracks so wide a goat could fall into them.

"Where could he be?" Jacob wondered. "I'm afraid he'll crawl into some hollow in the rocks and die."

"We can't search much longer," I answered. "The other goats still need us." Just then we heard moaning. It was coming from a boulder above us and it took a long while to climb up there. The Duke lay on his side, his yellow eyes wide with fear, his stomach bulging. I took off the canteen and Jacob held open the animal's mouth and poured all the water down his throat.

"Do you think we can find this spot again?" I asked. "I mean if we have to come back? The Duke is so heavy, even if we made a stretcher, I don't think we could carry him back to the clearing."

Jacob looked around for something to use as a marker and found one small twisty fig-pear tree. The fruit was gone now, but he took his shirt and tied it to one of the highest branches. Then, as we prepared to leave, we patted the very sick goat on his head.

"Should we say a prayer for him?" Jacob asked. This surprised me. We didn't come from a praying sort of family.

I had my own way of praying. It was like hoping with all my heart. Every night I tried to communicate with our parents. I sent my thoughts out into the universe.

"We are here. We love you. Come and find us." But I left God out of it, because I really didn't know how to think about God.

"Ok, you pray." (What could it hurt? I was interested in what Jacob would say.)

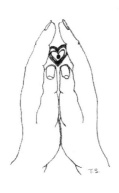

He pressed his little hands together under his chin and I did the same. He took a big breath. "This is Jacob calling. We are in a spot here and our goat is sick. We have to leave him, but if there's anyone out there who could help, we'd appreciate it. Amen."

I smiled and shook my head. What a cool little kid.

The big male goat turned his yellow eyes up to thank us, but he was in very bad shape.

SILVER LINING

Back at the clearing things were improving. Some of the goats were on their feet. Again we went from animal to animal, giving them water. A few came over and drank from the bucket. A few had started going to the bathroom.

Piles of poop with red and blue plastic dotted the meadow, but it was good they were getting the bags out of their stomachs. Mother Goat was still standing by the stone cottage, so I took time to milk her and though I didn't get much, the nanny seemed better.

On the way back from the spring, Jacob muttered something. "What?"

"I said, I don't know why we can't get water out of the well instead of walking all the way to the waterfall."

I stopped in the middle of the trail. "What a simple idea. You're a genius. Why didn't I think of that? We'll take one of the boards off the cover, tie one of the buckets to the rope and drop it down." The first bucket came up clean and sweet. In half the time now, we could get around to all the goats!

Some were still not doing well. The largest goats were the sickest and recovering slowly. By nightfall we'd cleaned up all the chip bags in the meadow and we were too tired to go on. The littlest goats were now eating grass, but most of the nannies still looked very bad. King Billy continued to lie on the top of the cliff and The Duke was nowhere around.

"Jacob, do you remember Grandma Jean's saying 'There is no cloud without a silver lining?'" I asked as we rested on the cabin's stone steps. "It means that even bad things can bring something good. The silver lining in the Chip Disaster is learning that we can use the well to get water instead of walking all the way to the pool in the rocks."

In the morning, first thing, we went out to check on the goats and were happy to see that most of them were on their feet and grazing. King Billy was even strolling around with the herd, drinking from the bucket that we'd left near the well. Later, the Duke walked slowly into the clearing. He didn't look healthy, but at least he was moving. He collapsed near the porch and I brought him more water.

A few of the other animals still looked pretty bad, especially the little white kid with black spots we called Polka Dot. He was one of the twins we'd helped bring

into the world, but he'd never been very strong. Every hour one of us would bring water to Polka Dot and the Duke, but in the end, Jacob sat holding Polka Dot's head as he died.

"Helping a goat die, is like helping a mother goat have a baby," Jacob whispered. "You have to sit and pet them and make them feel safe." My little brother's eyes were red and I knew he'd been crying.

CHAPTER 22

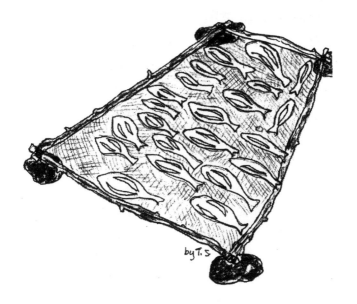

by T. S

THE GOOD DAYS

The days that followed were some of the nicest we'd had on Hope Island. The weather was pleasant and we had enough to eat. Each morning the sun rose and shone on the sparkling blue ocean. Little white caps dotted the waves. White seagulls swooped and dived above us. Some times it was so beautiful that I smiled and remembered what my father used to say. "No matter how troubled or down-hearted you are, there is always beauty if you look for it."

I was almost happy, even though I was lost on Hope Island and might have to live here forever. It made me think about my life before, how concerned I was about little things, like if everyone liked me or if I had cool clothes. None of that seemed important anymore. What mattered were the basics, food, warmth, Jacob and the goats.

During this time, even the fishing was good. Every time we went to the trap we came home with four or five fish. Once there were seven. We couldn't eat that many so I read up in the survival guide and attached what was left of the old netting to a frame and dried strips of fish on it. I even had some salt now to sprinkle on them.

Who would have thought of it, but Jacob? When he was out in the shed fooling around, he looked in the barrel we were using for trash and discovered that some of the old chip bags still had salt in the bottom. Carefully we emptied the grains into a jar and in the end we had almost half a cup of salt that we could use to sprinkle on the dried fish or put in the cheese, which made it much tastier.

Each night, as was our habit, when we got ready for bed, I would light a candle and read to Jacob. There were only four kids' books on the shelves and we'd read them all, but that didn't matter, we read them again. There was *The Little House on the Prairie*, *The Indian in the Cupboard*, *Charlotte's Web* and *Call of the Wild*. This last one wasn't really a children's book, but we read it anyway because it was about a wolf and we liked stories about animals.

There was another book I liked to read to myself, *Watership Down*. The words were too big for Jacob and because it was just for me, it was special.

What worried me was that the last two candles were getting shorter and shorter and soon would be gone. Then we would have no light, not for reading or even in an emergency. We could build a fire and sit around it outside, but inside the cabin the light from the cook stove would only dance on the walls.

Determined to solve the problem, I started going through the homesteader's books until I came to one I'd put aside the first day we came here, *Living on the Earth*. I liked the way the book started. "Hello Sun! You came up! We knew you would!"

It took me a long time to find a section on making candles. Meanwhile, I looked at drawings of hippies dancing and praying and building shelters and making necklaces and pickles. Some of the hippies were naked, but the pictures were nice and I didn't mind.

Our Grandpa told me once that Granma Jean had danced naked under the full moon when they were young and lived on a hippie farm, but he had a twinkle in his eye and I didn't believe him. Now I did.

Finally, I got to page 46. It showed ten different ways to make homemade candles. I chose the simplest.

How to Make Candles

First braid some cord.

I used some from the ball of twine we found under the bed.

The book said to braid it tight.

Then take some bee's wax and

slowly heat it in an old coffee can.

(Don't let it burn. Don't let it spill.)

While waiting, tie five braided strings to a short straight branch.

When the wax melts, carefully dip each strand in the can.

Over and over string by string, dip each one.

By the time you get to number five, number one will be hard,

then start all over with number one, dipping and dipping.

It takes almost all day, but by sundown you will have five new candles.

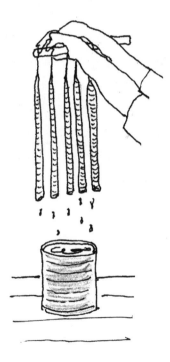

CHAPTER 23

by T.S.

COMING APART

FOR DINNER THAT NIGHT WE SAT ON THE STONE STEPS AND WATCHED THE SUN SET, FIRST PINK AND THEN RED AND THEN PURPLE. We built a fire and ate outside on the steps. All we had to eat was dried fish with raw greens and milk, but we were content.

As the stars came out one by one, Jacob rested his head on my shoulder, almost asleep. I thought how people say that the earth is warming up. Some scientists say we are doomed, but it's such a beautiful planet and I think things could change. People are smart and if everyone got together, we could adapt. We could use less electricity, gasoline and coal so there wouldn't be so much greenhouse gas, which is part of the reason the ice caps are melting. Look, at Jacob and me. We're doing ok.

Listening to the wind in the grass and feeling it on my skin, I felt a part of everything and I wondered if I had always felt that way. Probably not.

As we sat staring into the flames, Jacob broke the silence. "Remember the fight mom and dad had the day the sailboat sank?"

I looked at him, shocked. In all this time, the two of us had never talked about the terrible accident that changed our lives. We'd been too busy learning how to survive. Also the memories of those dark waters were so horrible I didn't want to relive them. Now Jacob was bringing it up.

"I was so scared," I answered him. "I thought we were going to die. I thought, this is it! This is what's going to happen to Trillium Stone. The next wave is going to pull her down and she won't be able to breathe and she'll struggle for a few minutes and then she'll be gone...

"Then I found you and held on to you like my arms were made of steel. I can't remember much else until I woke up on the beach. I know something hit my head and I wasn't right for a long time."

Jacob was poking the burning coals with a stick. His face was serious and the flames danced in his eyes. "I thought the same thing. I was screaming and crying, but I couldn't feel the tears because my face was wet from the salt water. Mom held on to my hand as long as she could, but the boat was going down and then the biggest wave came and I was swept away. I saw dad trying to get to us and then he was gone too. You were like my savior when you caught hold of me."

I put my arm around him, thinking he was going to cry, but he didn't.

"But I meant, do you remember their fight?" he asked "The fight about our family coming apart."

"What fight? What do you mean?"

"Don't you remember? Mom was mad because dad wanted to go on another nature trip to South America. Mom said she was sick of it, that she might as well not be married. She was tired of holding everything together while he went off on his jaunts having a good time. She was yelling at him."

I shook my head. "I guess my concussion was worse than I thought. None of this sounds familiar. None of it makes any sense. You aren't making this up, are you? Maybe you dreamed it."

"Trillium, you were there! You tried to get mom to calm down. You know how she gets. She threw her sunglasses at dad and they went in the water and you grabbed them out. This was before the big storm."

I had to face it. My little brother was telling the truth. The detail about the glasses was too real to be a lie or a dream.

"So what happened then?"

"Dad said he had to go on the trip. He was part of a team and it was his job. He said mom knew when she married him that traveling was in his blood and to go on this photo journey would be his greatest achievement."

"And mom... what did she say?"

"Nothing much. Just that maybe she shouldn't have married him then, if he cared more about his job than her."

I felt as if I'd been slapped. How could I not remember such a fight? Maybe I just didn't want to remember... or maybe it was the head injury. "Then what happened?"

"We just sailed around. No one talked and the wind got stronger and the waves bigger and then the dark clouds came. Big waves started coming into the boat.

Dad had to get the sails down and bail and Mom held on to us..."

"I remember that part for sure."

"But this is what I wanted to ask you," Jacob said, biting his lip. "Do you think Mom and Dad are still together or did they get divorced? There are lots of kids in my class that have two homes. Where would you want to live, with mom or dad?"

Now, I felt like crying. How could he ask such a thing? How could anyone choose? Both my mom and dad meant everything to me. They were the people who made me feel safe and loved.

"Oh, parents always have fights," I tried to make light. "They probably already got back together... Time for bed."

The fire was down to coals and I didn't have the heart to walk to the well in the dark for another bucket of water, so I took the house drinking water and threw half of it on the embers and watched the steam rise. It was like my heart was cut out of me. My heart.

RUNAWAY FIRE

That night Jacob snuggled against me under the covers and went to sleep right away, but I lay awake, thinking of what he'd said. It seemed impossible that our parents would even think of breaking up, but I knew Jacob was right. About half the kids at school lived with only one parent.

All this time, I'd imagined my mom and dad out searching for us, together. What if they were already separated? What if they were searching for their children alone and each blamed the other for the accident. Water came to my eyes. The thought of our parents being afraid and alone made me so sad...

I rolled over, adjusted the covers and tried to remember the good times... How our parents would goof around together. How they would smooch in the kitchen. How the whole family would watch TV together, like four sardines in a row, on their big bed.

Finally I fell asleep thinking those good thoughts, but in the night I had a bad dream. It was way too hot and I was wrapped in a sheet of plastic. I felt like I was smothering. The plastic crackled when I tried to get free... I woke hearing that word again.

DANGER, very loud and there was a rap on the door.

"Beeeeeyaaaa!" a goat cried. Something was wrong. I could hear the wind, but this wasn't unusual. On an island in the middle of the Pacific, the wind blew all the time, sometimes softly to amuse itself and sometimes so fierce, you had to bend into it just to walk.

Light flickered outside the window. When I opened the door, King Billy was running away. Then I saw flames.

"Jacob, fire!" With hands like claws, I shook him. "Fire!" Outside, the clearing was a sea of dancing orange.

I knew what had happened. Because I was too depressed to walk to the well to get another bucket of water, I'd not thrown enough on the campfire before bed. The wind must have blown sparks into the grass.

What to do! What to do! Ordinarily, I'm not the type who panics, but I didn't know how to fight a fire. There was no emergency 911 to call. We had no hose with running water. We had no fire fighting equipment.

Jacob was pulling his clothes and shoes on. "We have to get away! We have to get out of here!" he said.

"It's too late, Jacob. Look out the window. We're surrounded by fire! We just have to try to save the cabin and ourselves. The fire will burn out when it gets to the boulders... I'm going to take what's left of the water," I formed a plan as I dressed. "And run outside with the bucket and splash it on the wooden door and the shutters. You can help me. The stone walls won't burn and the roof's made of tin. The goats, hopefully, have all run away."

When we went outside, it was like stepping into an oven. First we splattered water on the door. Jacob looked like he was doing a wild dance, stomping on the little tongues of flame.

Then we closed the shutters and threw water at the wood so it wouldn't burn and melt the window glass. For a few moments the hot wind sucked the blaze away and we could look around. We were standing in a bowl of fire, like a crater in an erupting volcano and it occurred to me that maybe that's how Hope Island was formed... from a volcano. Then the wind shifted back toward the house and we ran inside.

All night Jacob and I lay together on the floor of the smoky cabin with the sheet over our heads. Outside the wind roared like a wild beast trying to get in.

"I hope the goats are safe," Jacob whispered in my ear. "Let's say a prayer for them."

"Ok, you say it."

"Dear God, Save our Goats. They are good animals and we love them. Amen."

I didn't understand much about God. Even when I tried to pray, I really didn't know what God was; not a stern man in a white robe with a long beard or a fat little Buddha fellow with a smiling face, I was pretty sure.

My Grandma Jean told me God was the sound of all

the hearts, of all the living things, beating... and not just of the living things but also the rocks and the sea.

My Grandpa said God was the sound of all the people singing. That sounded good to me, but how could you pray to all the people singing or all the hearts beating?

At first light, I got up, cracked open the door and peeked outside. We were still alive and unharmed, the stone cabin still stood and the wooden doors and shutters were only a little scorched.

Jacob and I tiptoed out on the porch to survey the damage. The sky was blue and the wind had blown away the smell of smoke, but the clearing was black. There were no flowers. No green grass. No friendly goats.

Later, when we went out to explore, we found that the well cover was gone, burned up in the firestorm.

The rope we used to pull up the bucket had burned. The boards we'd found on the beach and stored in a pile were gone, but the little goat's jungle gym tree still stood, only blackened at the base. That evening Mother Goat and her lady friends came to see us. Their udders were so full we got four jars of good milk. Then the goats went away. There was no grass to eat, not one green blade.

For the next few days, we had much work to do. We had to start carrying water from the waterfall pool again, until we could find a new rope. We went to the cove and brought back driftwood to make a new cover for the well so no goats would fall in. We continued to catch and cook fish, but there were no more campfires outside. We couldn't take the chance.

On the fourth day after the fire, it rained and on the seventh day, when we went out, there was the hint of green in the black clearing. The grass was growing back.

QUARREL

There were seventy-five marks on the walking stick now, fourteen new ones since the fire in the clearing. The grass was three inches high and the goats had returned. King Billy was again guarding the flock from the tallest rock and the little kids were playing on the jungle gym tree.

Jacob and I milked the nanny goats, morning and evening, as before. We carried water from the spring. We gathered wood. We hunted for greens. We checked to make sure the signal flags were still standing. We harvested the fish and on and on until it was time to go to bed.

If it rained or we were ahead of our chores, I would read or draw and Jacob would play with his pretend cars, but he complained all the time.

"How long do we have to stay here?" he whined. "Why don't mom and dad come? I wish I had ice cream. I wish I had orange juice. I wish I had my action figures." Finally I snapped. I had just had it!

"Well, we don't have any orange juice or TV so you'd better get used to it because we may be here a long time. We may be here forever!" As soon as I said it, Jacob's eyes filled with tears and I felt terrible. I put away my drawings and sat down on the floor to rub his back, but he ran outside crying.

Then I felt bad. I was a monster! I really was!

Jacob was brave and smart, but he was just a kid and he was even more scared and sensitive than I was. All day he didn't come back and when it started to rain, I went looking for him. In one of the caves at the edge of the clearing, I found him cuddled up with Mother Goat.

"I'm sorry," I said. "Don't worry about mom and dad. They're searching for us. It's just a matter of time."

Jacob wouldn't look at me and he didn't answer. He just rolled over and put his face in Mother Goat's fur, so I went away. That night I cooked a sweet stew of dried figs and honey, but Jacob didn't come to the cabin at dinnertime and though I meant to save it for him, I ate the whole thing.

CHAPTER 24

MOONLIGHT

SOMETHING WASN'T RIGHT. I'd fallen asleep and when I woke the full moon shone through the window. I moved my hand across the sheets and remembered that Jacob was mad at me and hadn't come home. I felt responsible. Maybe he was lying out there with the goats crying his heart out... or maybe he'd taken a walk in the dark and fallen into one of the huge cracks in the rocks.

Finally, I got up to get a drink of water and went out on the steps. Everything was washed by the moonlight. A mist rose from the ground and the shadows from the round silver moon stretched long across the clearing. So quiet. So beautiful, then a cry broke the silence. "Aieeeeee!" We'd heard that sound before and I knew what it meant.

A mother goat was trying to have her baby and things weren't going well. The goats made hardly any noise when the birth was normal. They just went away for a short while and then walked back to the clearing with one or two wobbly little kids.

"Jacob," I called, hoping he could hear me, but I didn't need to yell, he was already running toward the cabin.

"I heard it!" he said. "It's probably that fat goat, the one with the droopy brown ears that you said might be pregnant." His voice was high and excited. "Where do you think she is?"

"Not far. You get our birth supplies. I'll get dressed."

Jacob lit one of the homemade candles and stuck it in the lantern. Then he led the way, carrying the kit that I'd made for goat emergencies.

First we circled the meadow listening for her cry. Every few moments we heard it. "Aieeeeee!" But it was coming from further away. We followed the trail toward the beach as the sounds got louder and finally found Floppy Ears lying on her side in the middle of the path.

"Aieeeeeee!" She cried again and again as she strained to push her baby out, but nothing was coming. Two little feet and then a baby's nose should be showing. While Jacob held the lantern, I got down on my hands and knees and looked closer. All I could see was water dripping from the goat's backside, so the water bag had already broken.

"What shall we do?" asked Jacob in a low voice, careful not to scare the nanny. "Do you want to go in and feel around again?"

"I guess one of us should."

"You try," Jacob whispered. From our midwife mom we'd learned that it was important not to disturb a mother in labor or her contractions might stop. It was the same way with other animals, she said.

Jacob opened the birth kit, unscrewed a jar of water and poured it over my hands so I could wash. This time we had soap and I left some on my hands, like the goat book said, so they would be slippery. Carefully, I slid my right hand inside. What I felt surprised me. There wasn't a foot. There wasn't a head. There was a furry stub. The stub wagged, so the kid was alive.

"I felt it," I told Jacob. "A little goat's tail. Mom says when a human baby is coming with its bottom first it's called a breech delivery and they're more complicated. If you don't know what you're doing, the baby can get stuck and die."

"What can we do to help you Floppy Ears?" Jacob asked. The nanny strained and strained but nothing was coming. "Can you pull on its tail?"

I looked at him and laughed. "You're joking right?"

"Aieeeeeee!" cried the nanny struggling to stand up. We tried to help her, but she was too weak.

"We have to do something. Maybe I can find a way to get the legs out." I slowly slipped my hand back inside. This time when my fingers came to the tail, I moved past it until I felt a leg. Gently I pulled the leg to the left. Nothing happened. I had no clue what I was doing, but I tried pushing it to the right and the leg bent at the knee. Then I cupped the sharp edges of the little hoof and eased it down. "The first foot is almost out," I smiled at Jacob and he held the lantern higher so I could see.

"Can you get the second one?"

"Here it comes." Now two little legs were hanging out.

"Let's try to get her to stand again," Jacob suggested, so we both held her up and it was clear Floppy Ears felt better. "Beeeeeya," she said, meaning thank you and this time when she strained she meant business. The baby goat's back feet moved out a few inches. In the next push, the whole limp kid slid out on the grass.

"Whoa!" I yelled and looked away. The baby goat was covered with slime and blood, but Jacob knew what to do. With his bare hands he quickly pulled the membrane off the little animal's face, then he rubbed the baby with one of the rags we brought, until it made a weak cough.

"Is it breathing? Should I try to breathe for it?" I

was still looking away.

The baby goat sneezed and then sneezed again, clearing her airway. "I think she's going to be ok." Jacob pulled the little creature up to the mother's head where Floppy Ears went to work on it, licking and licking with her big quick tongue.

Soon the white baby kid was clean and it tried to stand up. This was the coolest part. The little baby goat got up and wobbled on its new legs to her mother. She was looking for food. Just moments after birth she was walking around.

"Let's call her Moonlight," Jacob whispered.

While the nanny nursed her new baby, we sat against a big boulder. We didn't talk. We just watched. I put my arm around my brother. We were lost on an island somewhere in the huge Pacific Ocean and we didn't know where our parents were or if they were even still together, but the big round moon shown down upon us. I loved my little brother. I loved the stars and moon. I loved Floppy ears and her baby.

Like Jacob said, we are goat midwives, I thought, but the goats are our midwives too. They take care of us and warn us when there's danger. They teach us things like where to find greens and fruit and water. They bring us milk. They give us comfort.

How to Make a Tin Lantern

Find a tin can.

Wash the can.

Get a nail or other pointed metal object like a screwdriver.

Pound holes in the tin can all around.

You can make pretty designs if you want to.

Make two holes near the top across from each other.

Put a piece of wire through the holes to make a handle.

Punch a bigger hole in the bottom of the can,

just the right size for your candle.

Stick the candle in the hole and light it.

Now you have a lantern if you have to go out in the night.

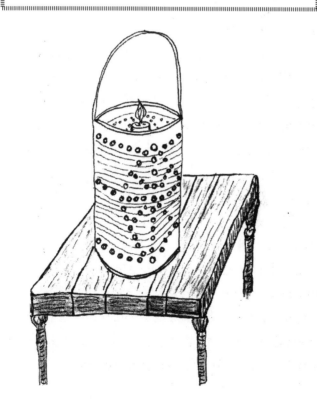

CHAPTER 25

RESCUE

For lunch the next day, I fixed figs with honey, the same thing I'd cooked for Jacob the night before. By afternoon, our chores were done and I was restless. Because of the quarrel we hadn't checked the flags or the fish trap. "Want to go down to the beach and swim and see if there are any fish?" I asked Jacob.

The afternoon was sunny and warm with small clouds that looked like white ponies dragging their tails behind them. Soon we were climbing down the cliff and running through the sand to the stone trap.

"Look, it's full of fish!" The pool churned with silver. Jacob started laughing and waded into the pool. "Wait. Don't get them excited. We have to harpoon them, one by one."

I got four and Jacob got five. He danced around the beach waving the spear with a wriggling fish on it. We took turns cleaning the fish, put them in our bucket and left the guts and heads for bait. Then, we played in the clear blue water.

With my eyes closed I called "Marco!" and listened for Jacob's answer. "Polo!" Then, still with my eyes closed, I had to catch him.

"Marco!" I called again and again.

"Polo."

"Marco!"

"Polo."

It was fun, but not as fun as when we played it with a bunch of kids at the community pool. That thought made me wonder if would ever see any of my friends again, especially Sebastian. Grandpa Pete, with a twinkle in his eye, asked if Sebastian was my boyfriend. "Noooooo!" I said.

That was ridiculous. Mostly ridiculous... though maybe I wouldn't mind.

Finally my brother and I turned for home. Half way up the cliff, something caught my eye and I stopped. At the edge of the horizon there was a white ship! It was only a dot, but it was getting bigger, coming our way. I put my hand on my brother's arm and pointed.

"A boat!" Neither of us moved, neither of us said anything, afraid to hope.

Then all at once we burst into action and scrambled up the rocks as fast as we could. At the top, we each grabbed a flag on a pole and started waving. Closer and closer the boat came. Though it still looked the size of a toy ship in a little kid's swimming pool, you could tell it was really a large pleasure boat.

"Do you think they can see us?" Jacob worried.

"I don't know. Wave harder!" So we did. We waved and waved... and waved...... and waved some more......... but the white boat didn't come any closer.

It was turning now, moving off at an angle, getting smaller and smaller and I realized, the island was probably surrounded by coral reefs and jagged rocks that could tear a ship apart. The captain didn't want to risk it.

Without a word, we picked up our bucket of fish and headed for home. Back at the clearing, the goats greeted us and wanted to play, but we weren't in the mood.

I built a fire, sprinkled four fish with salt and laid them in a pan of butter to cook. Jacob cut the rest up and laid them on the drying rack then he milked the nannies. Squish. Splash. Squish. Splash. There was no other sound but the wind.

When the fish were done, we ate our dinner. Then we went to bed and snuggled together. In the middle of the night, I heard Jacob crying. I held him tighter... then I cried too, but it was a silent cry. I didn't shake my shoulders. I didn't make a sob. I didn't want him to know.

DARK TIMES

In the days that followed, neither Jacob nor I mentioned the white boat, but everything was different. Before, it was like we were pretending to be Robinson Crusoe, just having an adventure until someone found us. Now we knew we really might be lost forever. We stopped going down to the beach to get fish or look for useful things that came in with the waves. We didn't even check the rescue flags. What was the point?

The lessons stopped. Jacob played with his cars while I stared into space. Sometimes, I read. The homesteader's books were all old and wrinkled, with pages that stuck together and smelled faintly of mold, but there were a few I liked, so just because I had noth-

179

ing else to do, I read them.

One thin blue book, *Jonathan Livingston Seagull* made me think about all birds differently. There was another I liked, *Uncle Tom's Cabin* about the slave days, but it was so sad. The third, *Watership Down*, was still my favorite.

Watership Down is a story about a group of rabbits whose home was destroyed and they had to find a new one. The rabbits in the tale seemed like real people and I could relate to their problems. You could tell the homesteaders liked that book too, because the binding was worn thin as if it had been read many times.

In a week, I finished all three books. Then I read *Watership Down* a second time and then there was nothing to do except work... pick greens, gather wood, make balls of cheese and milk the goats. I had to do almost everything while Jacob just played. He said he was on strike and then one night I'd had enough of him.

Outside the wind whined and a shutter slammed against the house, over and over, Bam, Bam, Bam. It was getting on my nerves. My little brother was on the floor with his white rocks playing cars in the candle-light and I kicked the cars as I walked by. It wasn't an accident. I just felt like kicking something.

"Hey, watch it." Jacob yelled.

"You watch it!" I yelled back.

Then he jumped up and pushed me so hard I fell back against the table and landed on my butt. It didn't really hurt, but it made me mad and when he laughed, that made me madder. I wasn't even thinking, but I crawled across the floor and grabbed Jacob's leg, got one of his sneakers off and threw it at him.

Now, the little kid's lips trembled and he looked scared, but I didn't care. I was sick of him. Sick of his baby ways. Sick of him not working as hard as I did. Sick of him whining. I looked around for something else to throw and saw the copy of *Watership Down* on the bed. It was a hardcover book and heavy.

SLASH! I flung it across the room. CRASH! It landed against the stone wall. Jacob ducked out the door and ran into the dark. He was crying now and I knew he would run to Mother Goat, but I didn't care. I didn't care if he never came back!

The beautiful old book with a picture of a rabbit on the front lay on the floor. My favorite book was now broken in half. Pages had come loose and were scattered around. The sight of the tattered book collapsed something in me. *Watership Down*, the book that gave me the most pleasure and comfort, was ruined by my own stupidity, my own bad temper.

I crawled over, took the pages and tried to put them

back together again, but it was hopeless and even if I had some tape it wouldn't have worked. The most I could do was arrange the pages in order and stuff them back into the binding.

I shook my head. It was all for nothing. Making the house nice, preserving food, trying to teach Jacob to read and do math so he wouldn't be behind when we got back to school. It was all for nothing. We weren't going to go back to school. We weren't going to see our mother or father or grandparents ever. The wind roared and bam, bam, bam went the shutter. Bam. Bam. Bam. Then the rain came.

I lifted my head and looked at the God's eye on the wall. Once I thought it was beautiful, now it looked faded and dirty and old. I looked at the curtains I'd washed and the wind chime made of seashells and our bed with the green patchwork quilt and I hated it all.

I wiped my eyes and wiped them again, but the tears kept coming. For the first time since we were lost on Hope Island I sobbed until I was choking, then I collapsed on the floor on my stomach and sobbed some more. Our situation was hopeless and I didn't care if I died right now. That's what I was thinking. I might as well...

I knew what dead meant. The end! I'd found my gold fish dead when I was seven, floating on top of the

water. It was stiff and fuzzy and had to be flushed down the toilet. I'd seen that first little goat die at birth. I'd seen the other little kid, Polka Dot, die after the chip disaster.

My brother and I would live on this island for the rest of our lives, alone and away from our parents. I'd never see Sebastian or any of our other friends again. We'd die of old age or starve to death or be killed in some accident and no one would ever know what happened. It didn't matter how many prayers Jacob prayed. If there was a God why did the terrible boating accident happen, anyway? Why did we lose our parents? Why did the white pleasure boat come so close and then turn away?

"Trill?" Lying on my stomach, I didn't even turn my head. It was Jacob at the door, peeking in to see if his sister was still acting crazy. He tiptoed in.

"Trillium, are you dead?" He said it that way on purpose, just like he'd said it months ago, the first day on the beach. "Trillium, are you dead?"

"Yes!" I said and he laughed and stretched out beside me on the cold floor. He put his arm over my shoulders. "Can we both play dead?"

I smiled. Jacob nuzzled up to me. "We're going to be ok," he said.

CHAPTER **26**

FALLING STAR

FOR A WEEK, MY BROTHER AND I WENT BACK TO DOING OUR BORING CHORES. We milked the goats and gathered food. We didn't fight and it seemed like Jacob tried to be more helpful.

To find wood, we had to go further and further from the cabin and we made a big pile. The sunsets were red and orange, even purple and the evenings were cooler, but we didn't go back to the beach where we'd seen the pleasure boat.

One night there was another big storm, this one far worse than the others, with lightning and thunder and a wind that roared. It roared so hard I thought it might blow the roof off, but the weather wasn't why we didn't go down to the cove. We just didn't have the heart for it. We'd lost hope. What if we saw another boat and it turned away...?

Finally we were sick of figs and milk, cheese and

greens for every meal.

"Let's go back to the sandy cove," Jacob said. "Our fish trap might be full."

"Ok," I answered without any energy. I really didn't care anymore.

Slowly, with Jacob leading, we wound our way toward the cliff. The afternoon was warm and breezy with big white puffs of clouds and a few of the little goats followed until we came to the drop-off.

At the top of the cliff, we stopped to look out across the wide ocean. Scanning for a boat or an airplane had become a habit, but as usual, there was nothing, nothing but the dark blue water, the seagulls and the wide, wide sky. When we got to the bottom, we were shocked to find everything a mess.

"Wow!" Jacob said.

I just stared. The fish trap was destroyed, all the rocks rolled away. The beach was littered with piles of trash. Seagulls and other water birds were fighting over the bones of a dead animal. There were small trees, with roots still attached, crisscrossed everywhere. The storm had brought in boards, pieces of plastic, even sheets of metal that looked like they were torn off a building. All this had been washed up on the big waves.

Jacob didn't seem to mind all the changes. He

thought it was beautiful. "Look," he yelled. "Look at all this good junk!"

"But the fish trap!" I moaned. "It took so many days to get it right."

"It's ok. I'll help you put it back together. We know how to do it now....This could be useful." He stooped down, picked up a board and dragged it up on the rocks where the waves couldn't get it. "Hey look a barrel! We could store stuff in that. Here's a rope. Now we can get water from the well again." In the end, I got inspired and helped him.

As we combed the beach we found a canvas tarp that could be used to improve the goats' shelters and a twisted piece of netting and two plastic water jugs.

After we repaired the fish trap, I felt better. We even discovered one lone fish still alive in the pool so we'd have something fresh for dinner.

"We'd better go. Soon the nannies will need to be milked." I looked up at the cliffs that were already in shadow then I picked up four boards from their pile and started to climb.

Jacob grabbed three smaller ones. "We found a lot of good stuff today," he said. Then he said nothing as we made the steep climb.

"Break time," I announced when we got to the top and we both flopped down panting.

Jacob dangled his tough little brown legs over the ledge. He was a nice little brother and I was proud of him. I reached over and tickled his ribs.

"You aren't so skinny as you used to be. You've got muscles."

I wanted to go home. I wished I could go home, but I knew now that we could make it on the island by ourselves, if we had to.

We had good food to eat. We had a sturdy cabin and warm blankets. We had our friends the goats and now we even had more boards if we needed to build something.

I stared out at the water.

The sky turned purple and then slowly dark blue, but I didn't move. Above us a field of stars took my breath away. I'd never seen so many stars, little diamonds of light, tiny suns. I lay back on the rock and pulled Jacob down with me, letting him use my belly for a pillow.

"You are a really cool kid," I told him... purposely not saying a "cool little kid." In the dark I could imagine his smile. "You're funny and strong and smart and brave." I stopped there, not wanting him to get too stuck on himself.

I squeezed my own arm muscle. I was different now too. I hadn't known I was changing. Once I was afraid of the dark and the sight of blood. Now I could walk around on moonless nights and help nanny goats have their babies. I could milk nannies and make cheese. I could make candles and build fish traps.

I thought of my mother and father and wondered again if they had drowned or been rescued. The sky was so big and so full of stars, the ocean so wide. Just a few days ago, when we had seen the white pleasure boat turn away, I'd given up hope and now here I was thinking about our parents again.

"But even if they're alive, how will they find us!" I said out loud and was sorry. I didn't want to upset Jacob again, but I needn't have worried. Jacob was asleep.

I let out my air in a long breath and just then the longest falling star I'd ever seen flew from one side of the dark blue sky to the other... My mouth dropped open.

Our dad had told us that falling stars were only bits of meteors that burst into flame when they neared the earth's surface... but for one to fall just then, of all times... just then, when I was thinking of our parents.

I closed my eyes and pictured the star falling in the great arc again. It could only mean one thing. It was a sign. Someone was searching for us. Maybe it was our parents, together or apart. Maybe it was our grandparents, but someone was searching... They wouldn't give up. I knew it for sure now. Someone would come.

THE END

AFTERWORD

"But what will happen? Are the parents really alive? Are they still together? Will they come? Will they find Trillium and Jacob?"

I'll tell you a secret. Trillium is right. The parents arc searching and the Grandparents too, but they're all looking in the wrong place. It will take a while longer and a stranger will come to the island first, but I can't tell you more. You have to read the next book in which Trillium and her brother will have more adventures, good times and bad times, but they will not give up hope again. And you dear reader should not give up hope either. Ever...

ABOUT THE AUTHOR

 Patricia Harman is a mom and a grandma who spent over thirty years caring for women and families as a midwife, first delivering babies in cabins and on communal farms in West Virginia and later as a nurse-midwife in teaching hospitals and in a community hospital birthing center. She has had a very exciting life and is now retired and lives in Morgantown, West Virginia, so she can write books for people like you.

When she was a kid, Patricia, (friends and family call her Patsy) liked playing outside and having adventures. She liked drawing and making up stories and putting on plays. She worries about wars and poverty and climate change, but she thinks if we all work together we can make the world better.

To contact Patricia Harman, email her at:
pharmancnm@comcast.net

To read more about her books, go to her website:
www.patriciaharman.com